CONSUMER
STOCK
MARKET

**DO NOT REMOVE
CARDS FROM POCKET**

1/4/94

ISBN:0-929230-13-2

Author: Marsha Bertrand
Editor:Marcia Castaneda
Contributing Editor:Charlene Brown

Book Trade Ordering:
PUBLISHERS GROUP WEST
4065 Hollis
Emeryville, CA 94608
1-800-365-3453
or
Ingram Book Company
347 Reedwood Drive
Nashville, TN 37217-2919
1-615-793-5000

To order a copy for your library:
QUALITY BOOKS, INC.
918 Sherwood Drive
Lake Bluff, IL 60044-2204
1-708-295-2010

If and only if, you cannot get the book at your favorite bookstore, you may order by sending address and money order/check for $8.95 ($5.95 + 3.00/shipping and handling). Send to: 4521 Campus, #388, Irvine, CA 92715. No credit cards/no phone orders.

YOUR BEST OPTION IS YOUR LOCAL BOOKSTORE OR LIBRARY. THANK YOU.

A Note From the Publisher—

. Two things motivated us to publish this book—1} the request from our many readers wanting a true consumer-oriented book on investing and 2} our own desire to publish a book that demystified investment terms and concepts. I feel, that more than other book on the bookstore shelf, Ms. Bertrand's book accomplishes both.

You will find that investing really is basic finance despite the investment world's effort (much like the legal world) to create the image that their profession is just too sophisticated for the consumer. *Nonsense.*

Consumers have also come to realize that savings and loans or banks may be no more safe than stocks. In this book there is an extensive demonstration showing how to research a company before you buy stocks. There is still no replacement for your own homework—who better to judge what, where, and how, your money should be invested?

In regards to choosing a responsible investment, it is becoming more and more popular to research a company's policies. In my own personal investments I am very concerned about putting my money with companies that share my particular beliefs. (There are a number of watchdog organizations that can assist you in your decision). I see this not only as a matter of personal ethics but as smart investing. We have seen how class action suits can cause a stock to drop dramatically. It seems to me, wise to invest in companies that are making every effort to stay around for generations by maintaining a high standard of ethics.

Whatever your personal objective, we know you will find this book a perfect guide for making your investments.

Please, use it well.

Charlene Brown

This book is dedicated to my husband, Gary, who gave me the encouragement, the confidence, and the opportunity to tackle this project.

My thanks to the Naperville Writers Group for their weekly critiques and support.

TABLE OF CONTENTS

CHAPTER ONE

WHY INVEST: RISKS AND REWARDS

Congratulations! You've apparently made the decision to begin investing your money in the stock market. You'll find you have some exciting prospects ahead of you! On your way to becoming a seasoned investor, you will no doubt experience the thrill of a stock's price quickly moving up right after you've purchased it. No doubt you'll also experience the frustration of a stock's price sinking as you receive your buy-order confirmation. Hopefully, the thrills will far outnumber the frustrations, and your investment dollars will grow.

Since you've already made the decision to invest, you probably have some specific reasons in mind for wanting to enter the market. Maybe you have visions of increasing your savings tenfold, or maybe you simply like the excitement of "playing the market." Whatever your reason, you'll have a lot of fun with it, but before you begin, it's important for you to be aware of the potential risks and rewards that await you. In other words, why invest?

SHARE PRICE APPRECIATION

The primary reason people invest their money in the stock market is share price appreciation (also known as capital gain). This term simply refers to an increase in the price of a share of stock. For example, let's say you buy one share of Clunker Car Company today for $10.00, and during the next week the company's stock price goes up to $15.00 per share. If you sell your share of stock, you've made $5.00 on your $10.00 investment—a return of fifty percent. That's share price appreciation.

Share price appreciation (also known as capital gain).

Unfortunately, while share price appreciation is the biggest potential stock market investing reward, there is also something called share price depreciation (also known as capital loss), which ranks as the number one potential risk.

Let's say that instead of increasing to $15.00, the price of that share of stock you bought for $10.00 decreased to $5.00 during the week. You now sell your share for $5.00. You've just lost half your original investment. Thus, the risk!

So if it's that easy to lose half your investment, why would anyone choose to put their money in the stock market when they could put it into a virtually risk-free bank account? The answer to that question lies in the relationship between risk and reward. While no investment is totally risk free, some offer less risk than others.

Typically, the higher the potential risk, the higher the potential reward. If you place your money in a bank account you'll have very little risk and will probably receive a guaranteed, although lower, percent interest rate. However, if you place those same funds in the stock market, while the risk may be greater, so is the return potential.

For example, let's say you buy a stock and its price increases by twenty percent. The risk you assumed by buying the stock paid off with a much higher return than the almost risk-free bank account. Once again, however, it's important to remember that the market works both ways. If the price of your stock had decreased, you would have been better off with the bank account that may have paid only five or six percent.

Of course, no profit or loss is realized on a stock until it's sold. If the price of your $10.00-a-share stock decreases to $3.00 a share but you don't sell it, you haven't lost anything. Conversely, if that stock rebounds to $15.00 a share and you don't sell it, you haven't made a penny. Therefore, if the current market price of the stock you own is higher or lower than the price you paid for it but you don't sell the stock, you have what is called a paper profit or paper loss, respectively. Real profits and losses are only realized upon the sale of the stock.

So, how do you know which stock will increase in price and which stock will decrease in price? Is it possible to know which way a stock is going at a specific point in time? The honest answer is a resounding NO! And anyone who claims to be able to predict stock prices is either lying or is in a deluded state of mind. There are, however, certain indicators that can be studied to get a feel of a stock's direction. By studying the particulars of a specific company, you can develop a somewhat educated guess as to how that company's stock will perform. But those techniques will be covered later. Back to the risks and rewards.

DIVIDENDS

Another reward of entrusting your money to the stock market is dividends. A dividend is an amount of money the company derives from profits and decides to pay its shareholders. Dividends are much more predictable than share price appreciation and depreciation. Most dividend-paying companies like to maintain at least a stable, and hopefully, an increasing stream of dividend payments. But do all companies pay a dividend on their stock? Absolutely not.

Whether a specific company pays a dividend is up to its Board of Directors. Instead of paying a dividend to the shareholders, the Board may feel it's more important to keep that money and use it to buy additional equipment or hire more people so the company can grow. Or maybe the company is barely surviving and can't afford to pay a dividend.

Whatever the reason, the payment of a dividend is left to the discretion of the company's Board of Directors. They are free to begin or stop paying dividends as they see necessary.

Therefore, a company that has never paid a dividend may suddenly decide to start paying out part of its profits, while a company that has paid out dividends for years may suddenly decide to keep those funds within the company.

Again, you never know for sure, but if you study the particulars of a specific company, you can probably get a pretty good feel as to what the company will do over the next several quarters.

Typically, most dividends are paid in cash; however, a company has one other option when it comes to dividends, that is, to pay a stock dividend. If the company chooses to pay a stock dividend, you, the investor, would receive additional shares of stock instead of cash. Just like with the cash dividend, the amount of stock given to each shareholder would be based on the number of shares the investor owns.

One thing to keep in mind about stock dividends, however, is that while it gives the investor the impression of receiving additional equity in the company, in reality, the investor's position remains the same.

For example, if there are 50 shareholders and they each own 100 shares of stock, that means there are a total of 5,000 shares of stock outstanding. Therefore, each shareholder owns 2% of the company (100 shares divided by 5,000 shares). Now, let's say the company pays a stock dividend of 10 shares to each shareholder. Now each investor owns 110 shares of stock and the total number of shares outstanding increases to 5,500 (50 shareholders times 110 shares each). Each shareholder still owns 2% of the company (110 shares divided by 5,500 shares). While everyone got extra shares, no one's ownership position changed. That is called dilution of the stock.

PSYCHOLOGICAL REWARD

Another reward people receive for entrusting their money to the stock market is the psychological reward. Through their investment they are helping to create jobs, produce products and services, and help stabilize the economy. While this reward certainly doesn't directly translate to money in the investor's pocket, it can create a sense of contribution.

EXCITEMENT

And lastly, people receive the reward of excitement when they invest in the stock market. Basically, investing is almost a form of legalized gambling. Will the price soar after you purchase the stock or will it drop to its lowest level ever? Or maybe it will remain at the price you paid. Who knows? That's the gamble and the excitement.

Now that you know the potential risks and rewards of investing, let's go back to the original question: Why invest? The real reason people invest in the stock market is to make money while exerting very little physical energy. Sometimes it works; sometimes it doesn't. The important thing to remember is that there is money to be made and money to be lost. You could be a candidate for either. With that in mind, if you're still willing to put your dollars into the stock market, it's time to decide how many you want to invest.

Typically, it's not wise to use your rent or mortgage money, car payment money, or grocery money for stock market investing. The money you invest should be funds that are left over after all your bills are paid. It should be money that, if lost, will not affect your standard of living. This is not meant to scare or intimidate the new investor; it's simply meant to remind that money can be lost. You don't want to have to go hungry because General Motors had a bad year. Start conservatively, get the feel of the process, and build from there. Investing in the market can be fun and exciting if you are cautious and prudent. With that in mind, set your investment dollar limit and step into the world of Wall Street.

CHAPTER TWO

HOW TO INVEST: CHOOSING A STOCKBROKER

You're now aware of the risks and rewards of stock-market investing, and you've determined how much money you want to initially invest. Now what? How do you get those extra dollars into that Chrysler stock? Do you call Lee Iacocca? Not quite. Only under very limited conditions do companies sell their stock directly to investors. Typically, if you want to buy stock, you must do so through a stockbroker.

To give you an idea of the stockbroker's purpose, let's look at the history of their job. In 1291, Teodisio d'Ora and a group of friends got together and decided to attempt to sail around the southern tip of Africa to find a new route to the East where the spice trade flourished. To do this, they needed money and therefore sought out financial backers (investors) and sold them shares of stock in the venture. The shares they sold were negotiable so that when a person no longer wanted to be an investor in the venture, he could simply sell his shares to someone else.

As people began to buy and sell the shares, a local coffee house came to be a meeting place where people would go when they wanted to buy or sell stock. If a buyer was at the coffee house when there were no sellers, he would

9

inform the waiter of his interest, and when the next seller came to the coffee house, the waiter would give him the potential buyer's name. Soon it became common practice for the waiters, to keep lists of potential buyers and sellers, number of shares available, and prices offered. When investors wanted to buy or sell, they simply checked with the waiters who would put them in contact with the appropriate person. Thus, the beginning of the modern stockbroker!

So seven hundred years later, you want to invest in the stock market. But where do you find a stockbroker today? Anywhere! They advertise on TV and radio. They run print ads in newspapers and magazines. They're listed in the yellow pages. Your co-worker knows one. Your neighbor works for one.

Soon it became common practice for the waiters to keep lists of potential buyers and sellers, number of shares available, and prices offered. Thus, the beginning of the modern stockbroker!

The real question is: how do you choose the right one?

The first thing you need to know is that there are two different types of brokerage firms: full-service and discount. To determine the difference between the two, let's look at each one separately.

A full-service brokerage firm is exactly what its name implies—full service. They offer their customers an array of amenities. When you use a full-service brokerage firm, your account will be assigned to a specific broker (who may be called an account executive or registered representative).

There are two ways to
slide easily through life;
to believe everything or
to doubt everything. Both
ways save us from thinking.

Alfred Korzybski

This person will assist you in building and monitoring your stock portfolio. For instance, say someone told you that Clunker Car Company is a good stock, but you don't really know what the company does, if it's profitable, if it pays a dividend, etc. All you need to do is tell your broker that you're interested and he or she will get literature and information on the company for you. The broker may even be able to give you specific information regarding the company, such as they've developed a new product or they have a division they're closing down.

But how would the stockbroker know that information? Full-service brokerage firms employ full-time analysts whose job is to research and analyze companies' stocks. These analysts determine if a certain stock is best to be bought or sold at a specific point in time. The firm then makes available those analysts' reports to their customers to choose which stocks to buy or sell.

When using a full-service firm, your broker will also work with you to help determine which stock is most appropriate for your investing strategy. He or she should be able to make specific recommendations. In addition, after you have purchased stock, the broker should continually monitor your stock portfolio. If a stock you own begins to decrease in price, and the brokerage firm's analyst believes it is going to continue to drop, your broker should inform you of the analyst's opinion. Obviously, the broker and the analyst, just like everyone else, cannot predict the market; however, they are available to give you their expert opinions. Whether you accept their advice is up to you. It's your money that's being invested, and you always have the final voice in determining how it's done.

The second type of firm is the discount brokerage firm. The door was opened for the emergence of this type of firm on May 1, 1975, when the Securities and Exchange Commission mandated an end to all fixed commissions. Unlike the full-service firm, the discount firm is strictly in the business of placing buy and sell orders for their customers. They are not in the advice business. They employ no analysts; they make no recommendations; they do not monitor a customer's portfolio. When you do business with a discount brokerage firm you are on your own as to what stocks to buy and sell. You must do your own research and make your own investment decisions.

Because discount brokers offer so few services, it's fairly easy to get into the business. Therefore, many banks and other financial institutions have begun offering brokerage services at a discounted rate. The primary discount brokerage firms, however, are independent firms that offer only brokerage services. They typically identify themselves as "discount" through their name or in their advertising.

The reason for the difference in the level of service between the full-service and discount brokerage firms—cost. Each time your broker transacts a stock purchase or sale for you, you are charged a commission, which is simply a fee for the broker's services. Because the full-service firms offer so many additional services, their commission charges are higher than those of the discount brokerage firms. For instance, if you buy a hundred shares of Clunker Car Company stock at $10.00 per share, the discount firm may charge you $35.00 to $40.00, while the full-service firm may charge you $50.00. Therefore, when choosing between full service and discount, it's simply a decision as to whether the extra service is worth the extra charge. Do you need a broker's advice and recommendation in choosing a stock, or would you prefer to choose your own? Do you need a broker to monitor your portfolio, or will you follow its progress yourself?

Once you've decided which type of firm you want to do business with, it's simply a matter of choosing the specific one you prefer. A personal recommendation from a friend is helpful. If you don't know anyone who works with a brokerage firm, you might want to stick to one of the major, more well-known firms. It's not that a lesser-known firm is not good, but despite the rules and regulations that govern them, a few less-than-reputable firms do pop up.

13

You may want to choose three or four firms that you would like to work with, then call and request literature from each of them. After reading through the material, pick one or two you prefer. Once you've narrowed it down to a couple firms, call and arrange a face-to-face meeting with the broker who would be assigned to your account.

Typically, firms will offer prospective clients a thirty-minute free consultation.

When meeting with the broker, he or she should ask about your needs and investing goals. If, instead, the broker tries to sell you something before discussing your investment strategy with you, go to the next firm on your list.

You should also ask for client references. Obviously, you won't be given the names of dissatisfied clients, but if the broker can supply you with the names of at least one or two happy clients, it's a positive sign. And lastly, check the broker's and the firm's credentials.

Contact your state securities commission. They can tell you if there have been any disciplinary actions taken against the broker or the firm.

You can also write to the Securities and Exchange Commission's Freedom of Information Branch in Washington, DC, for information as to any federal records of complaint. Once you feel comfortable that the broker and the firm are reputable, you're ready to open your account.

If after working with the firm a while, you find you're not satisfied, you can always switch your account to another firm. Or if working with a full-service firm, simply requesting a new broker at the same firm may resolve the problem. Remember, your broker should be willing to spend a reasonable amount of time with you and should be able to explain, to your satisfaction, any transaction made for your account. As with any other relationship, finding the person you feel most comfortable working with is the key to your satisfaction.

If you've decided you want to use a discount firm, be sure to compare prices when doing your research. Some of the discounters offer commission charges that are only twenty percent less than those of the full-service firms, while others offer commission rates that are up to seventy percent less than their full-service counterparts. In fact, some discount firms are beginning to increase their commission rates and offer additional services. Some discounters even offer gimmicks, such as a "round-trip discount," which is an additional discount from the regular commission charged if you both buy and sell a stock through the firm within a certain time frame—often sixty days. Therefore, since the level of service and the commission charges vary so widely from one discounter to another, when looking for a discount broker, it's important to do a little comparative shopping to make sure you're getting the most for your money.

So now you know you need a broker and you know how to find one. Let's say you're in the process of selecting a brokerage firm, and you're reading the literature you received from three different firms, when you suddenly get a telephone call from Jack Black, a broker with Black Brokerage Services.

Broker Black tells you, "I got a new stock that's so hot, I'd hate to see you miss out on it. Right now it's selling for only $3.00 a share, but it's a new company that's on the cutting edge of technology. It's a sure bet that the stock's going to go up to at least $20.00 or $25.00 a share within the next six months. It's virtually a no-risk investment. But if you want to get in on this great stock, now is the time to do it. Get in on the ground floor before it's too late!"

Here you were, looking for a broker, reading through brochures, and all of a sudden, right on the phone, you've got not only a broker, but a broker with a hot tip! Are you lucky or what? Probably "or what" if you agree to Broker Black's proposal. Be very wary of brokers with "no-risk sure bets". As we learned in Chapter One, there's no such thing as a no-risk investment. It's also not a sure bet that any stock is going to rise in price. When someone offers you an investment that's "no-risk" and a "sure bet," and puts pressure on you to buy right now before you "miss out", hang up the phone and go back to reading the literature you got from the well-known, reputable firms. It doesn't make sense to get involved with someone who isn't going to play fair with you.

Of course, that last statement is appropriate not only to the investor, but also to the broker. For instance, what's to stop an investor from opening two accounts—one with a full-service firm and one with a discount firm, then taking advice from the full-service broker and making trades through the discounter. Hopefully, your honor and sense of fairness will keep you from employing this tactic. It's basically stealing from the full-service broker. Besides, after giving you several recommendations and never having you authorize any purchases, the broker will catch on quickly. And it doesn't make sense for a broker to get involved with someone who isn't going to play fair. If you're going to invest, decide which type of brokerage firm you prefer and play it straight.

Choosing the right broker is an extremely important part of investing your money. You have certain needs and specific goals you want to accomplish. Make sure the firm and the broker you choose enhance your chances of achieving the success you want.

CHAPTER THREE

ESTABLISHING AN ACCOUNT

You've gone through the exercise of choosing the brokerage firm with whom you want to do business. Before you can begin buying and selling stock, however, there is paperwork to be completed and a few more decisions to be made.

THE PAPERWORK

First, the paperwork. You'll have to fill out some sort of standardized form requesting information such as name, address, phone number, and other essential details. In addition to these general information questions, you will also be asked specific questions such as your income level and net worth. This information is obviously very confidential. However, these questions are asked for a specific purpose. It is due to Rule 405. Rule 405 is an ethical concept set forth by the New York Stock Exchange stating that all brokers must "know their clients," because an investment that is suitable for one client may not be appropriate for another. A broker must obtain specific facts regarding a client's security holdings, financial condition, and objectives. Article 3 of the National Association of Securities Dealers (NASD) Rules of Fair Practice states that:

In recommending to a customer the purchase, sale, or

exchange of any security, a member shall have reasonable grounds for believing that the recommendation is suitable for such customer upon the basis of the facts, if any, disclosed by such customer as to his other security holdings and as to his financial situation and needs.

In 1987 the U.S. Supreme Court upheld the clause found in most brokerage agreements prohibiting customers from suing brokers.

The purpose of this rule is primarily to protect the broker from fraud or other unlawful acts by the investor, such as free riding, which is an illegal investment practice of purchasing stock, but not paying for it. Once the stock is purchased, if the price increases before the investor is forced to pay for it, he or she sells it and pays the broker, making a profit without investing a cent. If, however, the price of the stock decreases, chances are the investor will vanish or maybe argue that the order was never issued to the broker to buy the stock in the first place.

Of course, the investor also has protection from fraud by the broker. In 1987, the US Supreme Court upheld the clause found in most brokerage agreements prohibiting customers from suing brokers in court but, instead, allowing them to arbitrate their differences.

So, what if you tell your broker you want to invest $2,000 in the stock market and the broker suggests a particular stock that he feels would be a good investment.

You agree and authorize the purchase. A week later the price declines and you lose half your investment. Do you go to arbitration? Certainly not. The broker didn't put you into an investment that wasn't within your means. You are protected from being persuaded to invest more than you should in a risky investment, but not from losing money on an investment that is within your investing power.

Obviously, however, for both your and the broker's protection, while you're not expected to supply your broker with a dollar-for-dollar schedule of your finances, you should willingly and honestly supply the information requested. It's for everyone's protection.

What's money? A man is a success
if he gets up in the morning and
gets to bed at night and in
between does what he wants to do.

Bob Dylan

When setting up your account, your broker may ask if you want to open a discretionary account. In establishing this type of account, you give your broker power of attorney to make all buy and sell decisions for you. A discretionary account obviously puts a real burden of responsibility on the broker. Therefore, some will not even accept discretionary accounts. Typically, they prefer to give the investor advice, then work from the investor's specific instructions. Because a discretionary account gives your broker full control over your investments, it is not advisable to establish one with a broker you have just begun doing business with. This type of arrangement should only be made with a broker that you have done business with for an extended period of time and whom you trust fully. Even then, you should be careful in giving power of attorney to your broker. Once again—no one should have more power over your investments than you do.

THE DECISIONS - TYPE OF ACCOUNT

When opening your account, there are several decisions you will have to make. First, what type of account do you want to establish? Some of the more usual choices are as follows:
> Individual
> Joint Tenants with Right of Survivorship
> Tenants in Common
> Community Property
> Custodian

Let's look at each option and determine what it means.

INDIVIDUAL

If you will be the sole owner of the stock you plan to purchase, then you would open the account in your name only, which is called an individual account. The account and any stock certificates issued will appear with your name only.

Your stock portfolio will simply be regarded as an asset and in the event of your death will be part of your estate, which means that in your will you can bequeath your stock portfolio to whomever you wish.

JOINT TENANTS WITH RIGHT OF SURVIVORSHIP

If you are opening your account with a spouse or one or more other persons, you will probably set up your account as joint tenants with right of survivorship, which is the most common form of joint accounts. Through this type of ownership, each person listed on the account owns an equal share of all securities purchased. The account and any stock certificates issued will appear with the full names of all owners and will be followed by JT WROS (joint tenants with right of survivorship), or simply by JT TEN (joint tenants).

Under this type of ownership, when one joint tenant dies, his or her portion of the portfolio automatically becomes the property of the surviving joint tenant(s), thus, right of survivorship. The estate of the deceased person has no claim on the portfolio; therefore, with a JT WROS account you cannot bequeath your stock portfolio to anyone in your will because it automatically goes to the remaining joint tenant(s).

TENANTS IN COMMON

Another form of joint tenancy is Tenants in Common. This form differs from Joint Tenants With Right of Survivorship only in that the tenants or owners can own unequal shares of the stocks purchased. For example, if you and a friend open a Tenants in Common account together, you may own 60% and your friend only 40%.

The ownership doesn't have to be divided equally.

Also, under this type of ownership, if one tenant dies, his or her portion of the account does not automatically go to the other tenant. The deceased tenant's portion would be considered an asset and would become part of his or her estate, requiring the securities to be specifically bequeathed in a will.

COMMUNITY PROPERTY

In some states, property is owned jointly by a husband and wife by fact of their marriage. State laws vary, but in those states where community property laws apply, a husband and wife are considered to share equally in all of each other's property that is acquired during the marriage and in any income received or increase in value of assets occurring during the marriage.

CUSTODIAN

A Custodian account is one in which the actual owner of the account turns over its control to someone else—the custodian. This type of account is used with minors. It is set up so that an adult is the custodian and the minor is the beneficiary of the account. When the minor comes of age, the account then becomes his or her property. This type of account is also used for an Individual Retirement Account (IRA) because government regulations state that the owner of an IRA cannot control the account. Typically, the custodian of an IRA account is a bank, brokerage firm, or insurance company. Of course, with an IRA, the custodian usually charges a fee for its services.

There are, of course, other options in setting up your account, but despite all the options available, chances are, your account, as the majority of accounts, will be either individual or joint tenants with right of survivorship, depending on whether you open the account with a spouse. Once that decision has been made, it's on to the next.

THE DECISIONS - REGISTERED VERSUS STREET NAME

The next question to be answered is whether you want a registered or street name account. The primary difference between the two is that with a registered account you will receive a stock certificate from the company whose stock you purchase. With a street name account, a stock certificate will not be issued to you. Your ownership will be documented simply through book entry at the brokerage firm. The firm will then send you a monthly statement listing your holdings.

Let's look at some of the pros and cons of each option.

REGISTERED STOCK - PRO'S

The primary positive point in registering stock is comfort. When your stock is registered, the stock certificate is sent directly to you. You can see it; you can touch it. If there is ever a question as to your ownership, you have physical proof. In addition, if you decide to sell your shares, but you're unhappy with your current brokerage firm, you can take your certificate to any firm you like and have them sell it for you. If the stock is in street name, however, you would either have to sell it through the firm that's holding it or have that firm change it to registered stock so you could receive the certificate before you could sell it elsewhere.

Another advantage of having your stock registered is that the company whose stock you own will mail all materials such as annual and quarterly reports and proxies directly to you. This means that not only will you be assured of receiving this information, but you will receive it in a timely fashion.

REGISTERED STOCK - CON'S

As stated above, when stock is registered, the owner receives a stock certificate. That certificate is a negotiable instrument and must be handled with care. If lost or stolen, its replacement could be an administrative nightmare. In addition, if a missing certificate is not reported within a certain amount of time, you will be charged a percentage of the stock's value for its replacement. That charge can become rather steep when dealing with expensive or large amounts of stock. Therefore, if you choose to receive a certificate, you need to keep it in a safe place, preferably a safe deposit box, which creates an additional expense for you.

Another negative aspect of registered stock is its documentation and transportation. If you are holding your certificate and you decide to sell the stock, it is your responsibility to sign the certificate, have it signature guaranteed (in person at a bank, federal savings and loan, or by the broker), and then deliver it (in person or by mail) to your broker within five business days. This could be an inconvenience.

If you choose to do this, however, it's important to remember that if you send the certificate through the mail, you should send it registered, insured mail, return receipt requested (another added expense). By using this form of mail you will receive a receipt showing that the brokerage firm received the certificate. And if you don't receive the receipt, you'll know to follow up. In addition, if the package is lost, the certificate is insured.

STREET NAME - PRO'S

The primary reason people hold stock in street name is the ease of buying and selling. Here's how it works. Let's say you purchase a hundred shares of stock of Clunker Car Company in street name through the Alright

Brokerage Firm. You receive no stock certificate. Alright, however, will.

Let's say Alright purchased 100 shares of Clunker Car Company for you and 100 shares of stock for each of four other people. If all five investors purchased their stock in street name, Alright Brokerage Firm will receive a stock certificate for 500 shares from Clunker Car Company. The name on the certificate will be Alright Brokerage Firm.

Therefore, it is Alright's responsibility to maintain records as to who owns what portion of that 500 shares. Each month you and the other four investors should each receive a statement from Alright showing that you each own 100 shares of Clunker Car Company.

Because you have no stock certificate, if you decide to sell that stock, you can call your broker and he or she can sell the stock immediately. You don't have to worry about getting the certificate to the broker because the broker already has it. A quick call and your work is done. And in addition to the simplicity of the transaction, you also eliminate the expense of storing and mailing the certificate.

STREET NAME - CON'S

The primary problem of holding your stock in street name concerns the literature that companies mail to their shareholders. Let's go back to that 500 shares of Clunker Car Company that you and four other clients of Alright Brokerage Firm purchased. Clunker issued a certificate for

500 shares to Alright Brokerage Firm. As far as Clunker is concerned, Alright is the sole owner of that stock. They don't know your name or that you are a shareholder of their stock. Therefore, when they mail annual or quarterly reports to their shareholders, they mail one to Alright Brokerage Firm—the owner of 500 shares of their stock.

That certainly leaves you and your four fellow shareholders out in the cold. Luckily, however, knowing how the industry works, when Clunker mails literature to shareholders and they see Alright Brokerage Firm, they realize it is probably a combination of several street name accounts. Therefore, before they do their mailings, they contact each brokerage firm that holds street name accounts and ask them how many sets of materials they need to receive in order to supply one to each of their clients. In this case, Alright would tell them five, Clunker would send them five sets, and Alright would send one to you and each of the other four investors.

The procedure sounds simple, but there is one glitch.

Many brokerage firms never bother to forward literature to their clients—or if they do, it may take them several weeks to do it. Distributing company materials is not high on their list of priorities. Therefore, you, as an investor, may end up never receiving the information, or receiving it so late that the information is practically irrelevant. There is, however, a solution to the problem.

Most companies that issue stock maintain a mailing list

of interested parties to whom they send all of their regular literature. If you simply call or write to the company and ask them to put your name and address on their mailing list, you can be assured of having the information mailed directly to you. The only problem with this solution is that if the brokerage firm suddenly decides to start forwarding the literature, you'll then receive two of everything—but better two than none. You can always ask the company to remove your name from their mailing list, if need be.

One other negative aspect of holding your shares in street name is that you may not be able to participate in certain options a company may offer, such as a dividend reinvestment program or cash option payments. These items, however, will be discussed later.

So, the question is whether you want your account registered or in street name. If you want to hold your own certificate, and you don't mind the expense and responsibility of storing and transporting it, have your stock registered. If you'd prefer to have the brokerage firm hold your stock certificate, thus freeing you of the responsibility and making it easier to sell, then have the stock put in street name. It's purely a decision based on preference.

THE DECISIONS - CASH VERSUS DIVIDEND REINVESTMENT

Back in Chapter One we discussed that one of the rewards of investing is dividends—the portion of profits that some companies pay to their shareholders. Typically, companies pay those dividends on a quarterly basis. When setting up your account, you will need to make a decision as to how you want your dividends handled if you purchase the stock of a dividend-paying company. There are two options.

CASH

The first option is fairly straightforward. Each quarter the company will determine how much they will pay for each share of stock. If you own 100 shares and the company decides to pay $ .15 per share, your dividend will be $15.00. If you choose the cash option, you will receive a check for $15.00. If you prefer, you can give instructions to have the check sent directly to your bank to be deposited into your account, or you can have the check sent to the brokerage firm and have them hold the funds in your brokerage account. If you decide to have the dividend checks sent to the brokerage firm, the regular statement you receive from your broker should reflect the receipt of each quarterly dividend.

DIVIDEND REINVESTMENT

When you choose this option you are giving the company whose stock you own permission to use your dividend money to buy additional shares of their stock in your name. For instance, say your dividend is $15.00 and the current market price of the company's stock is $10.00 per share. The company will purchase 1 1/2 shares for you in your name. Many companies offer this service with no commission charge to the customer. Some companies even offer a discount on the stock price.

When you participate in a company's dividend reinvestment plan, you will receive from them each quarter, not a check, but a statement showing how many shares they purchased for you. The statement will tell you how many shares you received that quarter and will also give you the total number of shares you have purchased to date through the dividend reinvestment program. You will not receive a stock certificate for these shares unless you request one. If you want to sell your dividend reinvestment shares, you will typically have to ask the company to issue a stock certificate, then you will need to take that certificate to your broker to have the shares sold. Most companies cannot liquidate (sell) your shares for you.

You may have noticed that earlier in this section you became the owner of a half of a share of stock. Participation in a dividend reinvestment plan is practically the only way you can purchase a fractional share of stock. You could never ask your broker to purchase 10 1/2 shares of stock for you, but the company can credit your account with a fractional share. As they purchase additional shares each quarter, those fractional shares will grow to be full shares. When you ask the company to send you a certificate for your dividend reinvestment stock, they will send you a certificate for the total number of full shares and a check for any fractional share. For example, if the company was holding 22 3/4 shares of their stock for you, which was trading on the open market at $40.00 per share, and you requested a certificate, they would send you a certificate for 22 shares and a check for $30.00 (3/4 of $40). Certificates cannot be issued for fractional shares.

One drawback of participating in a dividend reinvestment plan is that the proper accounting for tax purposes can be a nightmare. It's important to keep track of the cost of shares purchased in the plan and the price at which you sell those shares, as you will have varying amounts of capital gains/losses on shares purchased at various times.

Dividend reinvestment is an easy and usually an inexpensive way of increasing the size of your stock portfolio. There is, however, one fact you should be aware of. Let's go back to our example. You have 100 shares of Clunker Car Company; they have paid you $.15 per share for the past three quarters. But their stock's price has fluctuated in the market so you have purchased the following number of shares:

Quarter 1: $15.00 dividend; $5.00 price = 3 shares.

Quarter 2: $15.00 dividend; $7.00 price = 2 1/2 shares.

Quarter 3: $15.00 dividend; $7.00 price = 2 1/2 shares.

Totals: $45.00 dividends, 8 shares

You now ask the company to issue a certificate for those eight shares so you can sell them. You get the certificate and take it to your broker, but in the meantime, the price of the stock has dropped back to $5.00 per share. Thus, you receive $40.00 ($5.00 per share x 8 shares) for the stock you purchased with $45.00 worth of dividends. You would have been $5.00 ahead if you had simply chosen to take all your dividends in cash. Of course, the stock price could have increased to $10.00 per share and you would have been far ahead. The point is, you have to remember that all the risks and rewards that apply to stock you purchase through your broker also apply to shares of stock purchased through a dividend reinvestment plan.

There is one other point that needs to be made regarding dividend reinvestment programs.

You may not be able to participate in the program if you are holding your stock in street name.

Remember, if your stock is in street name, the company doesn't even know you exist. Consequently, when they purchase shares for the dividend reinvestment program, they can't purchase stock in your name if they don't know who you are. Therefore, if you keep your stock in street name you will probably have to be content to receive your dividends in cash through your brokerage firm each quarter.

In summary, you can either have your dividend check sent directly to you or to your brokerage or bank account, or you can have the company keep your dividend money and buy additional stock for your account. Again, it is simply a matter of preference.

THE DECISIONS - CASH OPTION PROGRAM

Another option some companies offer is a cash option program. Through this program, if you are participating in the company's dividend reinvestment program, they will allow you to mail in additional cash contributions each quarter, and they will purchase extra stock for you. Let's go back to the $15.00 per quarter dividend you were receiving on Clunker Car Company.

As the quarter comes to a close, you realize you have an extra $60 in your checkbook that you would like to use to buy additional shares of the company. Instead of giving the money to your broker and paying commissions for the purchase, you can send the $60 directly to Clunker Car Company, and they will add it to your $15 dividend and purchase $75 worth of stock for you. The additional stock will be reflected on your statement and will be handled the same as dividend reinvestment program stock. Again, stock purchased through this type of program is still vulnerable to the same risks and rewards as the shares you purchase through your broker.

You have now given your broker general information such as name, address, and phone number. You've given the broker specific information such as your salary level and financial situation. You've decided what type of account you want to open, i.e., individual, joint, etc. You've decided if you want your shares registered or in street name. And you've decided if you want to receive your dividend checks or participate in the company's dividend reinvestment program.

Congratulations! You now have a full-fledged brokerage account. So what do you do with it? Read on!

CHAPTER FOUR

STOCKS: WHAT EXACTLY ARE THEY, AND WHY DO THEY EXIST?

You now have a full-fledged brokerage account, but before you go any farther, let's define exactly what these stocks are that you'll be buying, find out why they exist, and see how they differ from another investment offered by some companies.

When a company needs money, whether it be for day-to-day operations, to buy equipment, to build a new plant, or to add a new product line, it has two options. It can raise the money through debt (corporate bonds) or through equity (stocks).

DEBT (CORPORATE BONDS)

If the company decides to raise money through debt, it can borrow the funds from a bank or other lending institution, much like you would if you were taking out a home mortgage or a car loan. Or the company can borrow the money from individual investors, such as yourself, by selling corporate bonds to the public. Either way, the company will have to pay back the principal of the loan, along with a stated amount of interest, within a certain time frame.

Bonds are very different from stocks in that they do not offer the price appreciation and depreciation that exists with stock. When investors buy bonds they know exactly how much interest they will receive and when their investment will be paid back to them. If bonds are held to maturity, there is no question as to their performance, as long as the company issuing the bonds is healthy. Some bonds, however, are callable, meaning the company can redeem the bond after a certain amount of time. This happens when interest rates have dropped substantially and the company can borrow money at lower rates than they are paying on the outstanding bonds.

Bonds are very different from stocks in that they do not offer the price appreciation and depreciation that exists with stock.

When purchasing a bond, it's important to find out if it is callable so you will be prepared to relinquish it if necessary.

Besides being callable by the issuer, bonds can be sold by the holder prior to the due date of the loan. Only when an investor decides to sell a bond early does the value of the bond vary. That is because of the volatility of interest rates.

For example, let's say you bought a $10,000 bond that pays 9% interest ($900 per year) and will be paid off in ten years. The 9% the company agreed to pay you must have been the going rate at the time the bond was issued, or no one would have bought the bonds. But the bond has a life of ten years. What if three years after you bought it, interest rates in the marketplace go up to 10%? If you want to sell your bond you may have a problem, considering investors can get 10% interest on other investments and your bond is only paying 9%. Does that mean you can't sell it? No, it means you will have to sell it at a discount large enough to make the bond yield 10%.

Here's how it works. You're getting interest at the rate of 9% per year, which means you're collecting $900 per year (9% times $10,000). However, you now need that bond to pay 10% interest per year if you want to sell it. The only way that can happen is for you to reduce the price of the bond. At what price would you need to sell the bond so that the $900 you collect each year will represent a 10% return?

> **When purchasing a bond, it's important to find out if it is callable so you will be prepared to relinquish it if necessary.**

If you want to sell the bond in today's market, you'll have to sell it for $9,000 (10% times $9,000 equals $900).

Of course, the opposite of this scenario could also happen. If interest rates had declined, you would have been able to sell the bond for more than the original $10,000.

> **Remember, the rule is that bond prices always move in inverse relationship to interest rates.**

Another characteristic of bonds is that they offer investors a measure of security over stocks. If a company that has issued bonds has financial difficulties and ends up in bankruptcy, the bond holders will receive the repayment of their money prior to the stockholders receiving any funds. This gives bonds an edge of safety over stocks. Of course, if there is no money left to divide up in a bankruptcy situation, the bondholders could also lose their money.

Therefore, when purchasing bonds, investors should check the bond's rating. Ratings range from AAA to D, meaning the AAA is the safest, but probably pays less interest, whereas the D is the riskiest and probably pays a higher rate of interest.

There are several types of bonds available that have various nuances in regard to length of time, interest payments, taxability, etc. Investors who have an interest in bonds should consider the differences to determine which type of bond best meets their investing strategy.

EQUITY (STOCKS)

If, instead, a company decides to raise money through equity, it would do so by selling stock. This process is called an initial public offering (IPO). In an initial public offering, the company, through legal channels, creates stock, which is called authorized stock. The company would then sell either all or a portion of the authorized stock to the public, thus making the company a public company. The stock would be sold in increments called shares, and these shares would each represent a certain percentage of ownership in that company. One advantage an investor has by buying stock in an initial public offering is that the investor is charged no commission by the broker. Once the initial public offering is over, however, an investor purchasing the company's stock on the secondary market will be charged a brokerage commission.

When a company creates authorized stock, it may choose not to sell all of it in its initial public offering. Any stock that is kept by the company is called unissued stock, whereas any stock sold to the public is called issued and outstanding stock.

One advantage an investor has by buying stock in an initial public offering is that the investor is charged no commission by the broker.

Besides being a method of raising money, the option of selling stock also allows current company owners to "cash out" of their investment and sell part of their ownership to others. Of course, when they sell that ownership, as we'll see later, they also lose a portion of their control.

The price at which a company sells its shares in the initial public offering is set by the company and the brokerage firm (underwriter) that is doing the actual sales to the public. In setting the share price, they must try to determine how much investors would be willing to pay for each share of stock. The price must be fair or no one will buy the stock, thereby defeating the company's entire purpose.

> *Some see private enterprise as*
> *a predatory target to be shot,*
> *others as a cow to be milked,*
> *but few are those who see it as*
> *a sturdy horse pulling the wagon.*
>
> *Winston Churchill*

The company can sell as many shares it chooses. One company may sell one million shares while another may sell 250 million shares. As an example of how this works, let's say the Clunker Car Company sells 3 million shares of stock to 6,000 different investors at $9 per share. That means the company would raise $27 million (3 million shares times $9 per share). On average, each investor would have purchased 500 shares (3 million shares divided by 6,000 investors) at $9 per share, investing $4,500 each (500 shares per investor times $9 per share). While each investor owns 500 shares of the company, the company now has $27 million in cash.

But if the company is allowed to decide how many shares to sell and at what price to offer them, why wouldn't they sell millions and millions of shares at an extremely high price per share, thereby raising huge amounts of money? For the same reason you don't sell your $100,000 house for $4 million dollars. It's not worth it. Let's take another look at the $27 million the Clunker Car Company raised in its initial public offering. Instead of selling 3 million shares at $9 per share, why didn't they sell 4 million shares at $12 per share and raise $48 million instead of just $27 million?

Because they believe the investing public is only willing to purchase shares up to the amount of $27 million. This number is based on the company's current equity or assets plus expectations of the company's future earnings and growth, as investors not only base a company's value on the actual assets it owns, but also on its future income potential.

Some companies have even sold millions of dollars of stock to the public before they owned any assets or had one dollar in sales. Investors buy these shares simply on the basis of an idea.

To understand this, let's look at it on a smaller scale. Let's say you invent a device called the Mileage Augmenter, which, when attached to a car's carburetor, doubles its gas mileage. A car that typically gets 20 miles per gallon will routinely get 40 miles to the gallon with the Mileage Augmenter installed. You know the device works and you're certain that, if marketed correctly, you could sell millions of them. But there's one problem. In order to begin production on a large scale you need at least $100,000 to buy materials, hire personnel, and rent the space required for production. But you used up all your savings just developing and making the prototype of the Mileage Augmenter and you have no money left. So you go to your neighbor, show him your invention and he agrees to let you install it on his car for two weeks to prove to him it works.

Two weeks later your neighbor comes back, all excited about your new invention, and you tell him you'll make him a fifty percent partner if he'll finance the venture for $100,000. The deal is that he supplies the money and you do all the work. He agrees, and the two of you write a business plan. He gives you the money so you can start manufacturing the product, and six months later you're selling Mileage Augmenters as fast as you can make them.

So what happened here? All you had was an idea and a prototype of your invention. You had no inventory, no sales.

But you found an investor who was willing to invest $100,000 simply because he believed your idea had the potential of generating future income. It's the same thing when a company goes public. The investors don't only look at the assets and current sales of the company, they also look at the company's potential future earnings and growth. If they believe the company will grow dramatically, they're willing to pay a higher price for its stock.

Therefore, Clunker Car Company must set its initial public offering price at a level the investing public believes the company is worth. If they try to sell more stock than the public believes is the company's current and future value, no one will buy the shares, just like your neighbor was willing to invest $100,000 for the production of the Mileage Augmenter, but probably wouldn't have been willing to chip in $4 million.

else. This is called trading on the secondary market.

Let's look for a moment at how the secondary market works.

During the company's initial public offering (primary market), an investor bought 500 shares. The investor got the stock; the company got the money. A year later the stockholder decides not to keep the shares any longer and sells them to someone else (secondary market). The buyer gets the stock; the seller gets the money. What does the company get? Nothing! The company isn't involved in the transaction—only the buyer and the seller.

After the company has sold its stock to the public the first time in its initial public offering, it never gets another cent from those shares, no matter how many times they're bought and sold.

So if the company never again receives money from those shares of stock, why should management care if the stock is selling at $100 a share or $1 a share? For two reasons.

First of all, the people who are managing the company typically own shares of stock in the company. Often, they own fairly large amounts. Therefore, they have a personal interest in keeping the stock price as high as possible. When the stock price decreases, if they sell, they personally lose money.

The second reason management is concerned about the company's stock price is because what if three years after the initial public offering, the company has grown tremendously and sales are so good, they need to open another manufacturing plant. But the company's money is tied up in inventory and other capital assets, and they don't have the cash they need to establish another plant. So management decides to issue additional shares of stock to raise the money they need.

If you had bought stock from this company before for $9 a share, and the price then dropped to $1 a share, are you going to buy more stock from them when they offer it for sale again? Probably not. That's why it's important for a company to want its stock to sell at as high a price as possible. The existence of a strong secondary market makes the primary market work. Besides, increased shareholder value should be the goal of the company. That's why it is in business to begin with—to make money for the owners. And, of course, the owners are the shareholders.

But what if the company does extremely well and profits continue to grow year after year? What if profits are so good that the company increases its dividend every year?

What will probably happen is that everyone will want to own the stock, and the price will begin to steadily increase. But before long, the stock price has zoomed to $120 per share, and just to buy a round lot (100 shares) an investor would have to invest $12,000 (100 shares times $120 per share). Pretty steep for most investors. What can the company do so they don't lose the purchasing power of the average investor? They can authorize a stock split.

A stock split is simply an increase in the number of shares issued by a corporation without any change in its financial position. For every share of stock outstanding, Clunker Car Company could replace it with ten shares. Then, instead of trading for $120 per share, the stock would trade for $12 per share ($120 divided by 10 shares). The stock would be diluted. Clunker Car Company's total amount of stock would still be worth the same dollar amount, but there would just be more shares trading at a lower price. The average investor could then buy a round lot for $1,200.

In doing stock splits, the company can use any ratio in replacing shares as long as the dollar value of each exchange remains the same. In this example, they did a 10 for 1 split , but they could have done a 20 for 1, or a 2 for 1, or a 5 for 2. It's up to the company.

But what if Clunker Car Company shares had been trading at $1 per share, and investors were passing it over because of its low price? In this situation the company would do a reverse stock split. For instance, they may replace ten shares with one. Then each share would trade for $10 (10 shares times $1 per share). The total value of all shares would remain the same, but there would be fewer shares on the market.

There is one other option the company has if they want to reduce the number of shares available in the marketplace.

They could do a tender offer, in which they would offer to buy shares from current shareholders at a set price or they could simply purchase their own shares in the market just like any other investors would. Any shares purchased and owned by the company would then be called treasury stock.

> *Chances are, after purchasing this stock, the company would probably never resell it.*

In fact, if the major shareholders wanted to make the company private again so that they were the sole owners, they could simply continue to purchase shares in the open market until they had finally purchased all the available shares. Once again, the company would be a private company.

Now that you know a company has two options in raising money—debt (corporate bonds), which retains the company's private company status, or equity (stock), which makes the company a public company, let's look at the advantages and disadvantages of each method.

When money is raised through debt (corporate bonds), it eventually has to be paid back with interest, which, at times, could be a problem. At the same time, however, the company's owners don't lose any of their ownership. They still own 100 percent of their company and therefore have no obligations to outsiders.

If, instead, the company decides to raise money through equity (selling shares of stock), they don't have to worry about paying the money back. They do, however, lose part of their ownership and, in extreme cases, could even lose control of their company. In addition, once they have sold stock, they must regularly report to their shareholders the status of the company's operations and must even ask permission of the shareholders to make certain decisions.

As you can see, the two options are very different and present practically opposite sets of circumstances to the company. Therefore, when a company needs money, it's important that they look at both options and determine which is best for them.

Before we end this discussion, there is one other term you may encounter regarding private versus public companies.

That term is "closely held corporation." This is sort of a hybrid company in that it does indeed raise money by selling stock, but it sells its stock to only a very limited number of individuals. Typically, the stock of a closely held corporation is not traded on an exchange. Therefore, there is very limited change of ownership in the company's stock.

Now, back to the original question. What are stocks and why do they exist? A stock is simply a vehicle through which a company can raise money rather than simply borrowing it. When you purchase the company's stock, you receive part ownership of the company and derive certain benefits and rights.

CHAPTER FIVE

WHAT TO BUY: OBTAINING THE INFORMATION

You're all ready to make your first stock purchase but you find there are hundreds of stocks on the market. How do you decide which one is best for you? If you're working with a full-service broker, you can start by asking your broker's advice. He or she has access to analyst reports and should have some good suggestions. Of course being a professional still doesn't mean the broker can pick the money makers every time. So maybe you want another expert's point of view. If so, there are several investment newsletters published offering their author's opinions on the economy, the market and specific stocks. Most of these newsletters, however, are fairly pricey and must be purchased through an annual subscription. Therefore, if you decide to subscribe, choose one carefully, as some authors are self-proclaimed experts while others have proven their expertise over the years. If you find one you feel comfortable with, despite its cost, its purchase may be well worth the investment.

If you don't want to subscribe to a newsletter, there are several less expensive publications that can help you find the stock you want. Every major newspaper carries a business section that discusses the status of publicly-traded companies. There are a myriad of business magazines that offer investment suggestions, as well as television and radio programs that deal with stock market investing. When reading articles or listening to programs, watch for information on companies that are developing new products, opening new offices, or reporting higher profits than expected. When you read or hear something positive about a company, keep it in mind as a potential stock purchase.

You may find in your reading that certain stocks having specific similarities are categorized together. For instance:

✔ Penny stocks are stocks that are very low priced. These stocks are typically considered to be fairly risky.

✔ Blue chip stocks, on the other hand, are stocks that are considered to be of the highest quality and less risky. They are usually the stocks of stable, long-established companies that are leaders in their industry and have a history of good earnings growth and of paying regular dividends.

✔ Growth stocks are typically the stocks of young, fast-growing companies or stocks of companies that are in cyclical or very volatile industries. These stocks usually do not pay dividends, but offer good potential for stock price appreciation. Once again, many of these stocks are considered fairly risky.

✔ Income stocks are the opposite of growth stocks.

These are the stocks of established, stable companies in mature industries that have a history of paying a steady dividend stream. This term would be somewhat synonymous with the term blue chip.

Once you've completed your research and narrowed your focus to a few companies, you're ready to begin investigating each one.

The first thing to do is obtain the company's literature.

You can have your full-service broker do this for you or you can easily do it yourself. The address and/or phone number for most companies' corporate headquarters can be obtained from several reference books such as _Standard & Poor's Register of Corporations, Directors and Executives_ or the _Million Dollar Directory : America's Leading Public & Private Companies_ by Dun's Marketing Services. These and other similar publications containing this information are available in most libraries.

Once you know the address and phone number of the company's corporate headquarters, you can either call or write to their investor relations department. Simply state that you are a potential investor and want information regarding their stock. Ask specifically for the following items:

✔Most recent annual report

✔Most recent 10-K

✔Quarterly reports released subsequent to the annual report.

✔10-Qs released subsequent to the 10-K

Below is a description of each of these company publications.

Annual Report

The annual report is a booklet the company puts together each year to communicate to the investment community what happened during a specific twelve-month period (called the fiscal year). The book is typically divided into four separate sections.

1. Letter to Shareholders

2. Review of Operations

3. Financial Statements

4. Consolidated Footnotes

LETTER TO SHAREHOLDERS: This letter, which begins the booklet, usually discusses the company and its performance during the last year. The main topics include the company's annual sales and profits and why they are what they are. If the company did anything out of the ordinary during the year, such as acquire another company, move to a new location, develop a new product, close a subsidiary, or make a major increase or decrease in its employment force, these topics will be discussed in this letter. The letter should also contain information as to what management believes is the outlook for the future of the company. Finally, it is signed by the company chairman and/or president and often includes pictures of the signatories.

REVIEW OF OPERATIONS: This section will contain a description of the company's products and markets and should explain exactly what the company manufactures or sells or what services it offers. While this section is very public-relations oriented, much information can be gleaned from its pages. This section should include not only information as to what the company did during the past year, but also information as to what is planned for the future.

There are two times in a man's life when he should not speculate—when he cannot afford it, and when he can.

Mark Twain

FINANCIAL STATEMENTS: The financial statements represent the basic purpose of the annual report. Statements found in this section include the balance sheet, the income statement, and the statement of changes in financial position. Also included in this section is the Report of the Independent Accountants, also known as the Auditor's

Opinion. Typically, the accountants will issue what is known as an unqualified opinion. This opinion simply means the accountants agree that the financial statements present fairly the financial position of the company and the results of its operations in conformity with generally accepted accounting principles. This statement does not mean that the company's stock is a good or bad investment; it does not mean the company is doing well or poorly. It simply means that the information that appears in the annual report is presented properly to conform to proper accounting standards.

Sometimes the accountants will issue a qualified opinion when there are reservations about the statements, or if the accountant believes there may have to be a significant modification to the statements due to some expected development such as a pending lawsuit or possible tax liability.

Again, this opinion does not mean the company's stock is bad, but a qualified opinion should raise a red flag and prompt you to research the company more closely.

Two other possible types of opinion are the disclaimer of opinion and the adverse opinion. The disclaimer of opinion states that the accountants cannot give an opinion due to a restriction on the audit or uncertainty as to the accounts. The adverse opinion states that the financial statements do not fairly present the financial condition or the results of operations of the company in accordance with generally accepted accounting principles.

CONSOLIDATED FOOTNOTES: This last section of the annual report supports and explains the information that is presented in the financial statements. Some examples of what would be included are changes the company adopted in its accounting procedures, maturity of long-term debt and pending lawsuits.

Because each company has its own way of preparing an annual report, in addition to these four sections, you will probably also find various tables, graphs, and pictures sprinkled throughout the pages. Typically, the back cover of the report will include the names, and possibly pictures, of the directors, information as to the company's investor relations department, the company's address, phone number, stock symbol, etc.

When reading the annual report, it's important to remember that it was prepared by the company to be used as a communication tool for investors, analysts, brokers, and customers. Therefore, the narration will be presented in the most positive way possible. Even negative events will be described to sound positive in nature. When reading this report, concentrate on what is really being described and try to determine its real impact on the company. Some of the most important information in an annual report can be found by reading between the lines.

10-K

This financial report is also issued by the company on an annual basis. Unlike the annual report, however, it has no pictures, no glossy paper, no frills. The company is required to file this report on an annual basis with the Securities and Exchange Commission (the organization that polices the brokerage industry). In the past, information that was found in the 10-K was often not presented in the annual report; however, over the past several years annual reports have become fairly comprehensive and usually contain as much information as the 10-K. It's still a good idea, however, to obtain the 10-K and browse through it, as there may be additional information available in its pages.

QUARTERLY REPORT

This is an interim report that, once again, is prepared by the company to communicate to the investment community. The quarterly, however, discusses what has happened at the company during a specific three-month period and is therefore much shorter than the annual publication. Typically, the quarterly report is comprised of, first, a short narration of that quarter's sales, profits, and any other significant events that took place during the quarter and, second, the two primary financial statements, the balance sheet and the income statement.

Typically, the financial statements included in the quarterly report are unaudited.

10-Q

This report, like the 10-K, is a Securities and Exchange Commission filing. While the 10-K is filed once a year, the 10-Q is filed each quarter and covers a specific three-month period. Again, obtaining this report may present you with additional information that is not found in the quarterly report.

When requesting information from a company, these four publications are a must. In addition, companies may include copies of press releases, specials reports to shareholders or marketing materials. All of these materials will be helpful, but it's important to remember that many of these publications, especially marketing materials, are obviously written with a specific purpose in mind—to make the company look good.

Don't be impressed with glossy paper and lots of color. It's the words on the paper that are important.

CHAPTER SIX

WHAT TO BUY: ANALYZING THE INFORMATION

Now that you have all the reports you need, what do you do with them? The first step is to simply read through the written material. Begin with the annual report and read the Letter to Shareholders. Focus on items of company change, such as new divisions or products or large expenditures for new equipment. Read the section that describes the company's products and markets, and familiarize yourself with the company's operations and strategies.

Next, read the quarterly reports. Determine if any major events occurred during the quarters subsequent to the annual report that would have a major impact on the company. Then read through the 10-K and the 10-Qs to determine if they contain any interesting information that may have been left out of the annual and quarterly reports.

Now that you have digested the written material in the reports, it's time to tackle the numbers. Many times, annual reports will contain charts that depict important numerical data, such as sales, expenses, profits, or dividends, and will chart those numbers for a ten-year period. You can easily look across the chart to see if these numbers have increased, decreased, or remained stagnant over the past ten years, which will give you a feeling as to how the company has progressed.

The next step is to analyze the financial statements. Let's look at them one at a time.

BALANCE SHEET

A balance sheet is simply a look at the company's financial status at a specific point in time, usually the last day of the quarter or fiscal year. It tells you how much a company owned (assets) and how much a company owed (liabilities) on a certain day. It also includes the company's net worth, which is the amount of money investors have put into the company, plus earnings that have been kept in the company instead of being paid out in dividends. This is the amount of money the shareholders would divide among themselves if the company were liquidated at its balance sheet value. Typically , a balance sheet includes information for the current year or quarter and also from the previous year or the same quarter one year earlier. This is done so that anyone reviewing the balance sheet can compare the numbers from one period to the next. In addition, several important ratios can be calculated from the information presented on the balance sheet.

BOOK VALUE: This ratio is the closest actual value that can be placed on a stock. It is calculated by dividing the company's shareholders' equity (net worth) by the number of shares outstanding. This number is basically how many dollars' worth of equity the company has for every share of stock the company sold. Book value, however, has nothing to do with the market price of the stock, as many stocks sell at several times book value.

Let's take a look at the balance sheet for Clunker Car Company at December 31, 1992.

CLUNKER CAR COMPANY
December 31, 1992
Balance Sheet
(Dollars are in millions)

Current Assets	$ 1,177
Current Liabilities	720
Property & Equipment 968 Long-term Debt	175
Shareholders' Equity	1,250
Common stock, issued	113 million shares
Total	$ 2,145

At December 31, 1992, the Clunker Car Company reported shareholders' equity of $1.25 billion, with 113 million shares outstanding, which calculates to a book value of just around $11 per share ($1.25 billion divided by 113 million shares). However, Clunker Car Company's stock traded on the open market during the period October, November, December 1992, at a range from $33 to $36 per share—over three times its book value. When calculating book values, you will find that the stock price of some companies will be below book value, while other companies' stock will sell as high as thirty or more times book value.

So at what price to book value, range should a stock sell? While there is no definitive answer to this question, a guideline that could be used is how many times book value the average stock on the Dow Jones Industrials Average (DJIA) sells for at that particular point in time. This number can be found in several business newspapers, such as *Investor's Business Daily*. At the time Clunker Car Company's stock was trading at three times book value, the average stock on the DJIA was trading at 3.03 times book value, which was in line with Clunker's price to book value. It's important to remember that this comparison is of a specific company in a specific industry to an average of thirty companies, all in different businesses and operating in different environments. Therefore, this comparison is simply a general guideline.

Prayer beads work equally
well as technical analysis.

Quinn Waterloo

Another and possibly more meaningful way of using book value is to compare the book values of companies within the same industry. If the stocks of the DJIA sell at an average of 3.03 times book value, but most computer companies sell at ten times book value, that may be a characteristic of computer companies.

If, however, most computer companies sell at three times book value, but one sells at thirty times book value, this would be an indication that its stock is overpriced while the others are selling closer to their actual value.

CURRENT RATIO: This ratio determines the number of times the debt the company has that are due within one year (current liabilities) could be covered by the assets the company has that will be converted to cash within one year (current assets). It is calculated by dividing the current assets by the current liabilities, two numbers which can be found on the balance sheet.

For example, on December 31, 1992, Clunker Car Company had $1,177 million worth of current assets and $720 million worth of current liabilities. Calculating the current ratio ($1,177 million divided by $720 million) shows that the company has a current ratio of 1.6. This means that if the company had to pay off all its current debt with its current assets, it could pay them more than one and a half times. Obviously, the higher the number, the more solvent the company is, although too high of a current ratio may mean the company is not utilizing its cash resources very well. One way to determine if a company's current ratio is in line is to compare it to that of other companies in the same industry.

Another way to utilize this ratio is to calculate it for several years to determine if it has remained fairly stable or if it has increased or decreased. A decreasing current ratio could indicate the company is having money problems.

DEBT-TO-EQUITY RATIO: In the last ratio we looked at short-term debt—debt that must be paid within the next twelve months. Some debt, however, such as mortgages or loans may not be due for several years. These are called long-term debt. In the debt-to-equity ratio, the company's debt is compared to its shareholders' equity (the net worth of the company). This ratio can be calculated two different ways. It can be calculated using only long-term debt or using total debt.

Let's see where our example company, Clunker Car Company, stood on December 31, 1992. First, let's calculate the ratio using long-term debt only. On that date the company had long-term debt of $175 million and shareholders' equity of $1.25 billion. Therefore, $175 million divided by $1.25 billion equals .14, meaning that the company's long-term debt is only 14 percent of their net worth. Now let's look at the ratio using total debt. Total debt was $895 million, therefore, $895 million divided by $1.25 billion equals .72, meaning the company's total debt was 72 percent of its net worth.

As you can see from the difference in these two numbers, it's obviously very important to know which way the ratio was calculated when analyzing a balance sheet.

When looking at a debt-to-equity ratio, the lower the number, the stronger the company. A debt-to-equity ratio of 3.0 or higher may indicate that the company could have difficulty in financing additional growth, or it could even signify the beginning of a negative credit rating for the company.

INCOME STATEMENT

The next financial statement is the income statement. This statement describes how well the company performed during a specific period of time (one year for an annual report and three months for a quarterly report). It shows how much money the company took in (income), how much money the company spent (expenses), and how much money the company made (profit). This statement should also contain information from two consecutive periods. Again, several revealing ratios can be calculated from the information found in the income statement.

EARNINGS PER SHARE: Earnings per share (EPS) is a measure of how much money the company made during the year on a per share basis. It is calculated by dividing the net earnings (also called net income or net profit) by the number of shares the company sold (shares outstanding). Earnings per share is usually already calculated and stated at the bottom of the income statement. Let's take a look at the income statement for Clunker Car Company for the year ended December 31, 1992.

CLUNKER CAR COMPANY
Year Ended December 31, 1992
INCOME STATEMENT
(Dollars are in millions)

Net Sales	$2,468
Cost of Goods Sold	$1,280
Administrative Expenses	$ 523
Interest Expense	$ 42
Earnings Before Taxes	$ 623
Taxes	$ 247
Net Earnings	$ 376
Earnings Per Share	$ 3.33

As stated on the income statement, Clunker Car Company had earnings per share of $3.33, but let's see how that number was calculated. According to the income statement, Clunker had net earnings for the year of $376 million. We already know from the balance sheet that the total number of shares outstanding is 113 million. Therefore, $376 million divided by 113 million equals $3.33 earnings per share.

Now, what does this number tell you? It tells you that for every share of stock outstanding, the company made a profit of $3.33 during 1992. This money is free and clear and the company's Board of Directors must decide what to do with these funds. They may decide to use it to buy new equipment, hire additional people, increase your dividend, or they may choose to simply keep it in the company as a reserve.

But what if during the year Clunker Car Company had met with financial disaster and had lost money? Instead of net earnings, they would have had a net loss, and instead of earnings per share, the calculation would have created a negative number, or a loss per share. A major decrease in a company's earnings per share could be a signal that the company's operations are in trouble. In addition, if operations are poor, your dividend could be in jeopardy. When looking at a company's earnings per share, obviously, the higher the number, the stronger the company.

PRICE/EARNINGS RATIO: This ratio, often called the P/E ratio, uses earnings per share to show how much money the company is making compared to its market price. It is calculated by dividing the price of one share of the company's stock by the earnings per share.

Let's see how Clunker Car Company fared in 1992. At year-end the company's stock was trading at $36 per share. We already know that the company's 1992 earnings per share was $3.33. Therefore, $36 divided by $3.33 equals 10.8. This means that investors are willing to pay more than 10 times as much as the company is earning per share in order to buy its stock. Therefore, the stock is selling at 10.8 times earnings.

There are a couple of ways to look at a P/E ratio. A high P/E ratio may mean that the investment community believes the company has a bright future and will continue to grow and prosper, and that the marketplace believes future earnings will increase. On the other hand, a high

P/E ratio could mean that the company's stock is over-priced and very vulnerable. If a company with a high P/E ratio reports earnings that are lower than expected, or discloses a lawsuit it's involved in, or announces other negative news, investors may suddenly decide the company is not worth such a high price and begin to sell. When this happens, the company's stock price can fall several points, leaving investors with huge losses.

So what about the company with a low P/E ratio?

Does it mean that investors have no confidence in the future of the company, or does it mean that it is a strong company with lots of growth potential? That's basically a question each investor has to answer to his or her own satisfaction when analyzing the company's financial statements.

RETURN ON EQUITY: Return on equity is one more ratio that will give you a feel for how well a company is performing. This ratio is calculated by using numbers from both the income statement and the balance sheet. The calculation is simply net earnings (from the income statement) divided by shareholders' equity (from the balance sheet). This ratio gives you the return the company is realizing on its equity or net worth. A company is performing well if the return on equity is higher than current interest rates. If it is lower than current interest rates, that means the company could liquidate, invest the money in some form of financial paper, and make more money than they're making by operating the company.

Let's see what return on equity Clunker Car Company had in 1992. The company's net earnings were $376 million and its shareholders' equity was $1.25 billion. Therefore, $376 million divided by $1.25 billion equals 30. The company's return on equity is 30 percent—almost three times higher than current interest rates. Quite an impressive performance! Remember, however, this 30 percent represents what the company made per dollar of equity and is not what you should expect in dividends. Hopefully, a higher return on equity will be reflected in your dividend, but return on equity and dividend return are two different numbers. Again, this number can be compared to the return on equity number of other companies within the same industry to get a feel of the company's competitiveness in its own marketplace.

STATEMENT OF CHANGES IN FINANCIAL POSITION

This statement, also called a cash flow statement, is a repeat of the numbers from the other two statements. On this statement, however, the numbers are rearranged to explain the difference in the amount of cash and cash equivalents (investments, accounts receivable, etc.) the company has at the beginning of the year compared to the end of the year. It shows where the money came from and where the money was spent. Even though there are no additional ratios to be calculated from this statement, it should certainly be reviewed and not be overlooked.

When reviewing these three statements, one should also compare the numbers from the current year to comparable numbers from past years. In this way, any trends that are developing can be detected. Are sales increasing, decreasing, or remaining stagnant from year to year? What about expenses, income, or debt?

Detecting a trend of stagnant sales, decreasing income ,and increasing debt could make you turn to another stock for investment.

While the above ratios and calculations are some of the most basic and most widely used in analyzing a stock, there are obviously many other ways an investor can determine the viability of a stock. The ones presented here, however, are a good start in analyzing any stock.

FOOTNOTES

While the footnotes to the financial statements seem secondary, they are a very important part of gaining a complete picture of the company. As an example, let's say you're analyzing a company and see that the income numbers are as follows:

INCOME

1990	1989	1988	1987
$545,000	$279,400	$240,300	$204,300

The company's income increased by $36,000 (17.6%) from 1987 to 1988 and by $39,100 (16.3%) from 1988 to 1989, but suddenly increased by $265,600 (95.1%) from 1989 to 1990.

Did operations really improve that much? They certainly didn't.

In fact, operations were worse in 1990 than they were in 1989. If we take a look at the footnotes, we find that during 1990 the company sold a parcel of land it owned for a profit of $280,000. That means their 1990 income from operations, excluding the sale of the land, was really $265,000, ($545,000 minus $280,000), which was less than the $279,400 income reported for 1989. Their income from operations decreased by $14,400 (5.2%), from $279,400 in 1988 to $265,000 in 1990.

That additional $280,000 profit they received from the sale of the land is called an extraordinary item. It is not something that happens every year—it is a one-time sale of a parcel of land—an extraordinary item. Keep in mind, too, that an extraordinary item can affect the income in reverse. Income may appear extremely low one year. However, the cause could be due to an uninsured loss from a fire, or some other one-time event. Therefore, when looking at a company's income, it's important to take into consideration any extraordinary items that may affect it in a particular year. And that information is included in the footnotes. Hopefully, any extraordinary items that have a major impact on the company would also be discussed in the president's letter at the beginning of the annual report, but that doesn't necessarily always happen. You can be sure, however, to find that information in the footnotes.

Before we move to the next chapter, let's do a quick

review of the ratio calculations we've covered.

REVIEW OF RATIO CALCULATIONS

BOOK VALUE: Shareholders' equity divided by the number of shares outstanding.

CURRENT RATIO: Current assets divided by current liabilities.

DEBT-TO-EQUITY RATIO: Long-term debt divided by shareholders' equity
—or—
Total debt divided by shareholders' equity

EARNINGS PER SHARE (EPS): Net earnings divided by the number of shares outstanding.

PRICE-EARNINGS RATIO (P/E): Market price of stock divided by earnings per share.

RETURN ON EQUITY: Net earnings divided by shareholders' equity.

By no means does this list cover all the ratios that can be calculated when analyzing a company. Analysts spend a lifetime calculating ratios and analyzing companies' reports. The average investor, however, typically doesn't have the time or the patience to do an analyst's job. Of course, the more you analyze, the more familiar you will become with a company's operations, which will make you a better informed investor. As a start, however, the above ratios should give you a feel as to the strength of a company's financial condition.

Something else you may want to consider when analyzing a company is how much of the company's stock its management owns.

If this information is not included in the reports you have, you can request from the company a copy of their latest proxy, which will list each officer and the number of shares he or she owns. (The proxy statement will be covered in a later chapter.) If the top three executives of the company own 20% of the stock, that gives them real incentive to keep the price of the stock high. On the other hand, if they own 75% of the stock, they may have too much power. While there are rules and regulations in place that preclude their manipulating the stock's price in the marketplace, with that much stock, they do have the ability of making decisions without really concerning themselves with their investors' wishes. They may not care how investors vote on proxy issues because they already have the required majority of the voting power.

The type of analysis you just completed above is called fundamental analysis, as you are trying to predict the future movements of a stock based on an analysis of the company's balance sheet and income statement. You considered the company's assets, earnings, sales, products, management, and markets and determined from that information whether you thought the stock was under-

or over-priced at its current market value.

There is another type of analysis called technical analysis. This is the study of a stock's volume and price in the marketplace. Analysts use this information in conjunction with charts and computer programs to identify trends and predict a stock's price movements. Technical analysts do not concern themselves with the actual financial position of the company. Most technical analysis focuses on the short- or intermediate-term outlook of a security; however, some technicians also predict long-term cycles. Typically, individual investors analyze companies by using fundamental analysis rather than technical analysis.

Now that you've fully analyzed a few companies, it's time to make a decision as to which stock you want to buy and then, of course, make the purchase.

CHAPTER SEVEN

MAKING THE DECISION AND THE PURCHASE

MAKING THE DECISION

By the time you've completed the process of analyzing a few companies, you'll have a pretty good idea as to how a company is performing in relation to its current stock price. You'll have a notion as to whether the price is too high or too low compared to the company's operations. You may even have a feel as to whether the stock's price will increase or decrease based on the company's past performance. As you complete this process for several companies, you'll find yourself feeling much more comfortable with the performance of some companies over others. Those that you feel comfortable with are probably the ones you'll want to buy.

Once you have determined which company's stock you want to purchase, you must consider one other option. Many companies sell more than one type of stock. If a company sells stock, it must sell what is called common stock. Once again, common stock is simply a unit of ownership in the company. The people who buy the stock are partial owners of the company and have a voice in certain decisions regarding the management of the company and are entitled to dividends if the company chooses to pay out part of its profits.

Once the common stock has been sold, the company has an option of also selling what is called preferred stock. If you decide to purchase the company's preferred stock, you will no longer have a voice in the company's management decisions. However, your dividend and your investment will be more secure than that of the common stock owners.

With preferred stock, the amount of the dividend is set and does not change.

If the company has a bad year and does not have enough money left over to pay dividends to both the preferred and the common stockholders, the owners of the preferred stock will receive their dividend first. In addition, if the company goes into bankruptcy and liquidates, the owners of the preferred stock will receive all of their money prior to the common stockholders receiving theirs.

One of the funny things about the stock market is that every time one man buys, another sells, and both think they are astute.

William Feather

Some preferred stock is called cumulative preferred, which means that if the company cannot pay a dividend due to lack of funds in a specific year, the company's obligation to the preferred stockholders carries over to the next year, and they will receive two dividends before the common stockholders receive any dividend. In addition, some preferred stock is convertible, which means that after an investor has purchased it, he or she can convert it or exchange it for common stock.

So if common stock is riskier than preferred stock, why buy common stock? Remember the concept of risk versus return? Typically, the riskier the investment, the higher the return. While the preferred stock's dividend is guaranteed, it is also set at a certain amount and will not increase or decrease. The common stock dividend, however, can vary, giving the investor the potential of a higher return. In addition, the price of shares of common stock is much more volatile, giving the investor the potential of more share price appreciation.

One more thing to remember when determining which stocks to buy is that if you are buying more than one, it is probably best to diversify your purchases.

If your budget allows you to buy three stocks you could buy that of an automobile company, a pharmaceutical company, and a trucking company. Then if one of those industries has a crisis, you won't have all your investment money in an economically stressed industry. You don't want to be holding Chrysler, Ford, and General Motors stock when the auto industry has a major downturn. It's best to spread your investment dollars over a variety of industry stocks.

When investing your money you may also want to

consider your age. If you're young and still have decades until you retire, you may be willing to take a little additional risk because if you do lose money, you have plenty of time to replace it before retirement. Therefore, you may be more interested in a growth stock that pays no dividends but offers higher potential share price appreciation. On the other hand, if you are at or nearing retirement age, you may want to be slightly more conservative in your purchases. At this point in your life you don't want to lose the money you've saved all your life for retirement. Maybe an income stock that pays good dividends but offers less share price appreciation potential would be good for you. In addition, a younger person may want to reinvest all dividends back into the stock so that the portfolio will increase in size even faster, whereas a retired person may want to take those dividends in cash and use them for living expenses. Of course, these investing strategies are generalizations as to age groups. What's important is for each person to take into consideration his or her personal situation and determine the proper investing strategy for his or her own portfolio.

MAKING THE PURCHASE

You've reviewed the literature and calculated the ratios on three different companies, and you've decided you want to buy 100 shares of Clunker Car Company common stock. You check the newspaper and find that the stock closed at $35 1/8 the day before. But what is this 1/8? Stock prices typically increase and decrease in 1/8 dollar increments. The table below shows the conversion of those fractions into cents.

1/8 = 12 1/2 cents	5/8 = 62 1/2 cents
1/4 = 25 cents	3/4 = 75 cents
3/8 = 37 1/2 cents	7/8 = 87 1/2 cents
1/2 = 50 cents	

So, if Clunker Car Company's stock is selling at 35 1/8, it is selling for $35.125 per share. If it increases to 35 3/4, the price is $35.75. (Typically, when stock prices are quoted, such as 35 3/4, the dollar sign is omitted.) The price of some stocks is even broken down to sixteenths, but typically, the stocks you purchase will be reported in eighths.

Therefore, at yesterday's closing price of 35 1/8, your 100 shares would cost $3,512.50 (100 shares times $35.125 per share) plus commissions. The 100 shares you are buying is called a round lot. Round lot simply means 100 shares. Anything less than 100 shares is called an odd lot.

It's now time to call your broker. Let's say you get your broker on the phone and ask exactly what Clunker Car Company stock is selling for. He or she checks and tells you it's selling for an even $35 per share. Does that mean that you will buy it at $35 per share? Not necessarily. As you talk to your broker on the phone the price of the stock may go up or down. Five minutes later when the broker actually makes the purchase, the price could have changed even more. Therefore, there are a couple ways you can make this purchase.

First, you tell your broker to buy 100 shares of Clunker Car Company at the market price. This is called a market order, and it means that when the broker buys the stock, he or she will simply pay whatever the market price is at that time. Chances are that the price he quoted you ten minutes earlier hasn't changed, but if it has, the amount of the change would probably be minimal. You may have to pay slightly more or maybe you'll get the stock at a slightly lower price. Whatever, the difference should be fairly insignificant.

If, however, you want to buy the stock only at the exact price of $35 per share, you can give your broker a limit order at $35. This means that when the broker goes to buy it, if the price has increased to 35 1/8, the purchase won't be made.

Typically, a limit order will remain in place for just a day, unless you specify it to be good for a week, a month, or until canceled.

If the limit order is still in effect when the stock's price next hits $35 per share, the broker will then buy the 100 shares for you. (Once the stock is bought, the limit order is eliminated.) This procedure gives you the opportunity to buy the stock you want at the exact price you want.

There is one slight potential problem with limit orders that you should be aware of. In the scenario above, you told your broker to put in a limit order for 100 shares at $35 per share. The broker goes to buy the stock and finds the price is at 35 1/8 (12 1/2 cents per share more than you wanted to pay, making the total price $35.125 per share, or an additional cost of $12.50 for the 100 shares). Because the price is higher than $35, the broker doesn't make the purchase. During the next three months the stock's price continues to increase and eventually reaches $50 a share. But you don't own the stock. Let's look at what happened.

You wanted to buy the stock at $35 per share for a total cost of $3,500 ($35 times 100 shares). You could have bought the stock at $35 1/8 for a total cost of $3,512.50 ($12.50 more than you wanted to spend). At the end of three months the stock price is $50 per share; therefore, you could have sold your 100 shares for $5,000 ($50 times 100 shares), thereby making a profit (without taking commissions into consideration) of $1,487.50 ($5,000 sales price minus $3,512.50 purchase price). But you don't own the stock because you didn't want to spend the extra $12.50. You passed up the chance to make a profit of $1,487.50 because you didn't want to spend an additional $12.50.

While it's obviously important to set a limit on the amount of money you want to invest in the stock market, it's also important to be somewhat flexible when making your purchases.

Paying an extra eighth of a point may be worth the extra investment. However, straying too far from your set dollar amount of investment could be a disaster. Use your best judgment when making your investments.

Now, back to your purchase. Your broker tells you

Clunker Car Company is currently selling at $35 per share, and you authorize the purchase of 100 shares. The broker calls back 15 minutes later and says the shares were purchased at exactly $35 per share. Are you now the proud owner of 100 shares of Clunker Car Company? Not yet! You've made the purchase, and you've entered into a binding agreement to complete the transaction; however, in the brokerage business there is something called a settlement date.

The settlement date is always five business days after the trade date (the date the purchase is made). Therefore, if you purchased your stock on Thursday, February 1, you wouldn't be the actual owner until Thursday, February 8.

In counting the five business days, the day of the purchase and Saturday and Sunday are not counted. During that five-day period, your broker will require you to pay the total cost of the stock you purchased plus the brokerage commission.

So you did it! You acquired the information you needed. You analyzed the companies. You made your decision. And you bought the stock!

CHAPTER EIGHT

AFTER THE PURCHASE

Hello, shareholder! Welcome to the world of Wall Street! It's been three days since you purchased those 100 shares of Clunker Car Company, and when you checked your mail today you found an envelope from your broker that contained a single sheet of paper. This is your confirmation. It is simply a verification that the broker did, indeed, purchase the stock you requested.

The confirmation should include your name, address, social security number, and account number; the trade date and the settlement date; the name of the stock and number of shares purchased; the cost of the stock, the amount of commissions charged, and the total cost of the purchase. While you are not required to keep this confirmation, it may be wise to file it away, as it may come in handy as a future reference when filing your income tax forms. Remember, when you receive your next monthly statement from the brokerage house, you should once again verify that all business transacted during the month appears on the statement.

If you have your account registered in your own name, the next piece of mail you receive will be your stock certificate. Remember, the certificate is a negotiable instrument. Keep it in a safe place—preferably a safe deposit box. If, however, you've put your account in street name, you will not receive a certificate because your broker will hold it for you and the confirmation and subsequent statements will be the only evidence of ownership you'll receive.

Now that you are a shareholder, what should you expect? Does the company whose stock you own have any responsibility to you? They certainly do, just as you have certain responsibilities to the company. Let's first look at what's expected of the company.

> *Big shots are only little*
> *shots who keep shooting.*
>
> <u>*Christopher Morley*</u>

THE COMPANY'S RESPONSIBILITIES

The primary responsibility the company has to its shareholders is, of course, to perform to its highest potential and deal honestly with its customers, vendors, and investors. The obvious aside, however, the company's responsibility to its shareholders is to keep them informed. You've received your confirmation and possibly your stock certificate, but what other mail will you receive from Clunker Car Company? You will receive, at a minimum, five pieces of correspondence per year, and possibly even ten or more.

Public companies are required by law to send at least five separate items to their shareholders each year. (These items may come directly from your broker if your stock is in street name.) These five mailings will consist of:

✉ Annual Report: This report must be forwarded to you within 120 days (4 months) after the end of the company's fiscal year. Therefore, if Clunker Car Company's fiscal year ends December 31, the annual report should be in the mail to you by the end of April.

✉ Quarterly Reports: The company will also send you copies of their quarterly reports within sixty days after the end of each of the remaining three quarters.

✉ Proxy: Once a year the Clunker Car Company must hold an annual meeting. At the annual meeting shareholders are requested to vote on such issues as the election of the Board of Directors, the hiring of the outside accounting firm, and any other pending matters that require shareholder vote.

Because the annual meeting is usually held at or close to the company's corporate headquarters, and their shareholders are scattered around the world, many of the shareholders are not able to attend. So how can they vote?

All public companies use what is called a proxy. A proxy is an invitation to the shareholders to attend the annual meeting. The invitation includes not only the standard when and where, but also a discussion of the issues on which the shareholders will vote.

> *Included with the proxy is a proxy card. This card is basically a ballot on which you are to cast your vote.*

Your name and address and the number of shares you own will be printed on the card. The issues to be voted on will be listed with boxes next to each of them for you to record your vote. A line for your signature and the date will be at the bottom of the card.

Because it is difficult for so many of the company's shareholders to attend the meeting, this card gives them the opportunity to still participate in the decision-making process. It's important that you complete the card and return it to the company in the postage-paid envelope they provide as soon as possible.

Remember, if you want to attend the annual meeting in person, you are most welcome. In fact, it's a great opportunity to talk directly to management and ask them, face to face, any questions you may have. Even if you do attend the meeting, however, it's best that you complete the proxy card and return it beforehand so the votes can be tallied prior to the meeting.

So, the material Clunker Car Company is required to forward to you is the annual report, three quarterly reports, and an annual meeting proxy. Those are the five required mailings. There are, however, other mailings that you may receive. For instance, if the company pays a dividend you will receive five additional pieces of mail per year. What those pieces are will depend upon how you have your account set up. We will cover those mailings a little later in a discussion of dividends, but for now be aware that you will receive four dividend checks or statements per year (one after the end of each quarter), plus an IRS Form 1099-DIV, which is the tax form the brokerage firm is required to supply to you. This form will tell you how much you received in dividends during the year, which is the information the IRS will want from you when you file your taxes.

You're now receiving ten mailings a year in regard to your stock purchase: Annual Report, Quarterly Reports (3), Proxy, Dividends (4), IRS Form 1099-DIV. What else could you receive? There are a couple of possibilities. If a major event takes place at the company, management may issue a press release and send a copy of it to all their shareholders. Possible announcements made via press releases include earnings statements, change of management, and new products. Some companies also mail company fact books or annual meeting review letters, but basically, the ten mailings described above will probably be all you'll receive.

Now that you know what to expect in your mailbox, let's take a look at the company's responsibility in paying you your dividends. There are three possible ways for you to receive your dividends.

1 . If your account is registered in your name and you choose to receive your dividends, you will receive, directly from the company, four checks per year (one after the end of each quarter).

2. If your account is registered in your name and you choose to participate in the company's dividend reinvestment plan, you will receive from the company four statements per year (one after the end of each quarter). Each statement will include information as to how many shares were purchased for your account that quarter, at what price, and the cumulative number of shares in your account.

3. If your account is registered in street name, you will receive, not from the company, but from your broker, four checks or, if you made arrangements to have your broker deposit the dividends directly into your brokerage account, four statements, per year.

But exactly how does the payment of dividends work? Let's say you called your broker on March 1 and authorized the purchase of 100 shares of Clunker Car Company. On April 24, your neighbor, who is also a Clunker Car Company stockholder, stops by with the dividend check he just received from the company. Should you rush to your mailbox to see if your check is awaiting you? Don't bother. It won't be.

Before this seeming injustice can be explained, there are four terms you need to become familiar with—declaration date, record date, pay date, and ex-dividend date.

✔Declaration Date: This is the date when the company announces how much per share it will pay in dividends for that specific quarter. This announcement is usually released to the newspapers and brokerage community via a press release.

✔Record Date: Every company that pays a dividend must set a record date each quarter. The record date is basically a cut-off date. Anyone who owns the company's stock on that day will receive the dividend for that quarter. If you own the stock on the record date you are called a holder of record and are entitled to the dividend.

✔Pay Date: The pay date is the date the company puts the dividend checks in the mail or credits the shareholders' accounts with their dividend reinvestment shares. The amount of time between the record date and the pay date allows the company to collect data as to who is eligible for the dividend, to purchase shares for the reinvestment accounts, to print checks for the cash accounts, and to get the checks and statements in the mail. A pay date can be as long as 45 days after the end of the quarter.

✔Ex-Dividend Date: The ex-dividend date is the first day on which someone purchasing the company's stock would not receive the most recently announced dividend. Typically, a stock's price will move up by the amount of the dividend prior to the ex-dividend date, then fall by the same amount after the ex-dividend date.

Let's look at how this worked at Clunker Car Company. On February 10, management issued a press release announcing that on April 21, Clunker Car Company would pay a dividend of $ .45 per share to holders of record as of March 4. So what does that mean? It means the following dates apply.

Declaration Date: February 10
Ex-Dividend Date: February 28
Record Date: March 4
Pay Date: April 21

February 10 is simply the date they announced the amount of the dividend (the date of the press release). February 28 is the first day a new purchaser of the stock would not receive the dividend (remember, it takes five business days to settle a stock transaction). March 4 is the day you must be an official shareholder in order to receive the dividend. April 21 is the day the company will put the checks in the mail.

So why didn't you get the dividend?

You called and told your broker to buy the stock on March 1. Doesn't that make you a holder of record as of March 4, the record date? Well, no. You bought the stock after the February 28 ex-dividend date. Remember our discussion of trade dates versus settlement dates? It takes five business days from the day you have your broker buy the stock before your purchase becomes effective. If you bought your stock on March 1, you're not even an official shareholder until March 8 (five business days later). Therefore, even though you've owned the stock for a month and a half when the dividend is paid, you still don't get it. Seem unfair? Not really, when you consider why the system is set up the way it is.

First of all, on February 10 the company announced that the record date would be March 4. This gives everyone ample time to buy the stock and be a holder of record by that date. On March 4 the company has to determine exactly who their shareholders are, buy stock for those who are in the dividend reinvestment plan, prepare statements, write checks, stuff the statements and checks into envelopes, affix postage, and mail them.

Because of the amount of work involved, most companies hire a transfer agent. A transfer agent, usually a commercial bank, is an appointed representative of the company who maintains the records of shareholders, issues and cancels stock certificates, and resolves problems arising from lost, destroyed, or stolen certificates. One of the transfer agent's prime responsibilities is calculating and paying the dividend. No small task! It takes a long time to complete the dividend process. Thus, the April 21 pay date in the example above.

Despite the explanation, it probably still doesn't seem fair that you owned that stock for a month and a half and didn't get the dividend. There is, however, another side to the story. Let's try another example.

Let's say you've owned 100 shares of Clunker Car Company for a year and a half. The price has gone up and you have a tidy little profit, so you decide to sell your stock. On March 1 you call your broker and authorize the sale. Five business days later you are no longer a shareholder of Clunker Car Company. A week later you receive in the mail a check from the sale, profit and all. Is that the last you'll hear from Clunker Car Company? Nope! Come April 21 they're putting a dividend check in the mail to you. Even though you authorized the sale of your stock on March 1, you were still a holder of record on March 4, the record date. You sold the stock a month and a half ago but you're getting a dividend check anyway!

The moral of the story?

When buying and selling dividend-paying stock, it's wise to find out when the company's record date for that quarter is before you begin your transaction. Maybe by holding off your sale for a day or two you can collect an extra dividend.

Be careful, however, in doing this. It can backfire on you. For instance, if you own 100 shares of a stock that pays a dividend of $ .15 per share, which gives you a total dividend of $15 per quarter (100 shares times $ .15 per share). You decide you want to sell the stock because you bought it at $20 per share and it's now trading at $26 per share—a nice profit. But when you go to sell it you find that if you wait two days you'll still be a shareholder on the record date, so you decide to hold it an extra two days before selling in order to get the dividend. The next day the market opens and the price of the stock goes down $ .50 to $25.50 per share. By waiting to sell you've managed to get the $15 dividend, but you lost $50 in your sale price (100 shares times $ .50 per share). You would have been better off to sell the stock right away and forget the dividend.

Obviously, this is a judgment call on your part. You didn't know the stock was going to go down—it could have gone up just as well. The point is, don't buy and sell solely on the timing of dividends. It's something to keep in mind and consider, but it shouldn't be your entire focus.

There is one other responsibility the company has in relation to keeping its investors informed. While it's not a requirement, most public companies maintain an investor relations department. The people in this department are knowledgeable about the company and its stock. If you have a question about the operations of the company or about your stock, feel free to call or write to this department. It is their job to act as a liaison between the company and the investment community. Whether your question pertains to how they think their new product line will increase revenues, or you don't understand how your dividend was calculated, these are the people who can help you.

Keep in mind, however, any questions you ask must relate to information that is already public. They can't tell you that there's a contract pending to sell one of their subsidiaries if it hasn't been announced publicly. That would be inside information, which will be discussed in the next chapter. In addition, you can't expect these people to give you information that isn't maintained on a regular basis. If you want to know the average sales break-even point on a line of products that has seventy different sales prices, and this isn't information the company regularly maintains, forget it. They're not going to have an accountant spend half a day calculating numbers for a shareholder. Considering that most companies have hundreds of shareholders, they don't have time to do this. You'll find, however, that most investor relations people are more than willing to try to answer your questions.

That sums up the company's basic responsibilities to you as far as keeping you informed is concerned. But what about you? Do you have any responsibilities to the company?

YOUR RESPONSIBILITIES

Basically, the only responsibility you have to the company is to vote your proxy when you receive it in the mail. The company depends on your vote and you should take full advantage of your opportunity to be a part of the decision-making process.

You also have, however, a few responsibilities to yourself—primarily, to keep track of your stock after you've purchased it. It's not wise to buy stock then completely forget about it. You should follow its progress by reading the information the company sends you and by checking the stock price on at least a weekly basis. If the price is slowly dropping, you should want to know that before you've lost half your investment.

But how do you check the price?

Call your broker once a week? No need to do that. You probably have the price of your stock in your hand every day and just don't realize it. All stocks traded on a major exchange or market are listed in most daily newspapers. But exactly what is a major exchange or market? An exchange is simply an institution that provides the facilities for trading securities. The exchange does not buy or sell stock, nor does it set any stock prices. All trading at the exchanges must be done by an exchange member and all stock traded must be registered on that exchange. The two primary exchanges are the New York Stock Exchange (NYSE) and the American Exchange (AMEX).

The largest US exchange is the New York Stock Exchange (NYSE), which is also sometimes called the Big Board. This exchange transacts 85% to 90% of the total volume of business in listed securities. The NYSE was founded in 1789 as a secondary market where people could trade the $80 million worth of bonds the US government had authorized to finance the war. On May 17, 1792, 24 brokers signed the Buttonwood Tree Agreement, installing themselves as the first members of the NYSE and agreeing to charge their customers a quarter of a percent in commissions. The NYSE adopted a constitution in 1817, which has governed the trading of stocks for almost 200 years.

Today, in order to trade stocks on the NYSE, a person must become a member of the exchange, which is accomplished by buying a seat. The cost of an exchange seat continually varies but has ranged from $17,000 to substantially over a million dollars.

The second largest exchange in the US is the American Stock Exchange (AMEX) which trades the stock of more than 1,000 different companies. The AMEX was originally called the Curb Exchange, as it originated as an outdoor market located near Wall Street, where trading took place in the street. As on the NYSE, anyone wanting to trade stocks on the AMEX must become a member by buying a seat.

There is one other primary market which provides trading for stocks not listed on the two major exchanges. It is the National Association of Securities Dealers Automated Quotations, or NASDAQ, as it's commonly called. This market is what is called an over-the-counter (OTC) trading method, a term that dates back to colonial times when merchants sold the few securities that were available, literally over the counter like any other merchandise. Customers could purchase a bag of sugar, a pound of butter, and shares of stock in a local corporation.

While stocks are no longer sold in retail stores, the NASDAQ, unlike the exchanges, is not housed in a specific building.

The market is instead, basically, a telephone market to which brokers subscribe. The brokers then communicate bids and offers to each other via telephones and computers. The price of a stock you purchase over the counter is the result of a negotiation process between your broker and another securities dealer. Or the shares you buy may come directly from your broker's own inventory of stocks that he's purchased from other customers.

If you plan to trade stock that is sold over the counter, you should become familiar with two terms: bid and asked prices. The bid price is the price you will receive for your stock when you sell it. The asked price is the price you will have to pay for the stock when you buy it. There is typically a small difference between the two prices. That difference is called the spread. This spread may vary from a quarter of a point to a full point, depending on how actively the stock trades.

There is one other grouping of stocks, approximately 11,000 of them, that sells so infrequently that they are not listed on the NASDAQ computer system. These stocks and their bid and ask prices are listed daily on what are called the pink sheets. Typically, pink sheet stocks are the stocks of very small companies. The trades that take place in pink sheet stocks are very minimal. While the above are the primary U.S. stock exchanges, other smaller exchanges do exist in the U.S., and each has stocks that trade exclusively on that exchange. In addition, certain stocks that trade on the NYSE, AMEX, or over the counter can also be bought and sold on these other smaller exchanges. Chances are, however, that every stock you buy and sell will be traded on the NYSE, the AMEX, or over the counter. Now that you are familiar with the major U.S. exchanges, let's see how you can check the price of a stock that is traded on one of them. Let's say Clunker Car Company is traded on the New York Stock Exchange and you want to check the price. In the business section of most major newspapers will be a section called "NYSE Composite," or "New York Stock Exchange Composite Transactions," or something close to that wording. The stocks that are traded on the NYSE are listed in alphabetical order by a shortened version of their name. The stock you're looking for should be fairly identifiable. Here's the listing for Clunker Car Company:

52 Week						Vol.				Net
Hi	Low	Stock	Div.	Yld.	P/E	100s	Hi	Low	Close	Chg.
41	34	Clunker	1.80	4.9	10	102	38	36	37	+1/2

The first two numbers tell you that during the past 52 weeks (one year) the highest price that Clunker Car Company's stock sold for was $41 and lowest price the stock sold for was $34. The third column simply gives you the abbreviated form of the company's name.

The fourth column, which has the heading "Div.," tells you the estimated annual dividend which is based on the most recently paid quarterly dividend multiplied by four. If the company has a history of increasing dividends, this estimate may be low compared to the dividend the shareholders will actually receive. Because Clunker Car Company paid $ .45 per share last quarter, the reported $1.80 is calculated by multiplying $ .45 per share times four quarters.

Column five, "Yld.," is a calculation of the percent of return that the annual dividend represents. For instance, if Clunker Car Company paid $ .45 per share last quarter and its annualized dividend is $1.80, and if the current stock price is $37 per share, the dividend yield is 4.9% ($1.80 divided by $37).

It's important to keep in mind, however, that the yield stated in the newspaper is based on the current price.

In this example the yield is 4.9% because the stock closed at $37 per share. If you own the stock, however, and you bought it at $35 per share, your yield would be 5.1% ($1.80 divided by $35). Therefore, the yield listed in the newspaper may not be the same as a shareholder's yield because the newspaper always bases the number on the current closing price.

Column six gives the Price/Earnings ratio, the current price of the stock divided by the company's earnings per share.

Column seven, "Vol-100s," tells you how many of the company's shares were bought and sold on that particular day. The "100s" means that the number is reported in hundreds, which are round lots. Therefore, the 102 in the Clunker Car Company listing would mean that 10,200 shares of the stock were bought and sold that day. This number is typically referred to as the stock's volume.

Columns eight and nine represent the highest price the stock traded for and lowest price the stock traded for on that particular day. Clunker Car Company traded as high as 38 and as low as 36 that day.

Column ten gives you the close for the day. The 37 means that at 4:00 p.m. New York time, when the NYSE officially closed, the company's last stock trade was made at $37 per share.

And finally, the last column gives you the net change in the stock's price from the previous day. If, on Wednesday, the closing price for Clunker Car Company stock was $37 and the net change was +1/2, that means that on Tuesday the stock closed at $36.50 per share. If the net change had been -1/2, the stock would have closed at $37.50 on Tuesday. Many times you will hear the change in the price of a stock referred to as points. If a stock's price goes up one point, this simply means it went up one dollar. A dollar and a point are the same.

That is the basic listing you'll find in most newspapers. There are, however, various other letter codes you might see on a stock listing, such as an "x," which means the stock has gone ex- dividend. There are other codes that may reveal important information about the company, such as that it is in bankruptcy. These codes vary from newspaper to newspaper, but are always explained in a blocked off section of the page entitled "Explanatory Footnotes." It's important to pay attention to these footnotes and understand their meaning.

But what if Clunker Car Company had been listed on the AMEX instead of the NYSE? Then how would you read it? Exactly the same. The AMEX and the NYSE listings are presented the same way. But what if Clunker Car Company was traded over the counter on the NASDAQ? Some newspapers still present the listing almost the same way. However, others present a shortened version. For example, if you picked up a Chicago Tribune and looked up Clunker Car Company on the NASDAQ, you'd find the following entry: Stock Sales Last Change Clunker 102 37 +1/2. This tells you that 10,200 shares were traded that day, and the stock closed at a price of $37 per share, which was a $ .50 increase from the day before. Sometimes, the newspaper tables will list both the bid and asked prices of the stock.

You now know how to check the current price of your stock by simply leafing through the newspaper.

But what if you don't have a newspaper handy? Got a TV? With cable? There are cable stations that carry primarily financial news and run what is called a ticker tape across a small portion of the screen. A ticker tape is a continuous reporting of every stock transaction. The tape is divided into two bands, Network A and Network B. Network A reports all NYSE-listed securities transactions, while Network B reports all AMEX-listed and regionally traded securities transactions. The prices you see on the ticker tape appear in the order in which the trades are actually made and are presented only 15 minutes after the actual transaction is completed. Pretty up-to-date information! Subsequent to the close of the market each day, the ticker tape typically continues to run and shows the closing price of each stock for that day. When the market is closed, the stocks are listed on the ticker tape in alphabetical order.

So you decide to watch the ticker and look for Clunker Car Company. But all the listings are only a few letters long! That's because stocks shown on the ticker are shown by their stock symbol—a letter designation that each public company is required to have. The symbols for all listed stocks consist of three or fewer letters while the symbols for the over-the-counter stocks include four or more letters. For example, Hershey Foods, General Motors, and Ryder System, three NYSE-listed stocks, use HSY, GM, and R, respectively. Forest Labs, an AMEX-listed stock, uses FRX. MCI Communications and Oshkosh B'Gosh, two over-the-counter stocks, use MCIC and GOSHA. A company's stock symbol can be found in its annual report or in the Standard & Poor's *Stock Guide.*

Once you know a stock's proper symbol, it's simply a matter of finding those specific letters on the correct band of the ticker tape. For example, you look up the stock symbol for Clunker Car Company in the annual report and find that it is CCC. The stock is traded on the New York Stock Exchange, so you find CCC on the upper band of the ticker and see that the complete listing is "CCC 24 1/2." That means that 100 shares of Clunker Car Company sold for $24.50 per share. But what if the last transaction was for 2,500 shares at $23.50 per share? The ticker would then show "CCC 25s 23 1/2." If the number of shares traded is less than 10,000, the number is shown in round lots (100 shares). Therefore, 2,500 shares would be shown as 25s. If, however, the number of shares traded is 10,000 or more, the full number will be shown. For example, "CCC 11.500s 30" means that 11,500 shares of

Clunker Car Company sold for $30.00 per share. If the number of shares does not appear, the trade was for 100 shares. Odd lots are typically not shown on the ticker.

The above are examples of how a company's common stock would be listed. But what if the company also has a preferred stock? Preferred stocks are indicated by the letters Pr and are shown as follows: "CCC Pr 12.000s 24 1/2," which means that 12,000 shares of Clunker Car Company's preferred stock traded at $24.50 per share. The listing can even be broken down further to show that it was Clunker Car Company's preferred stock, Series E, which is a convertible stock, as follows: "CCC PrE.CV 12,000s 24 1/2." There are other additional codes that can be used on a ticker tape, such as RT for rights, WS for warrants, or XD to indicate ex-dividend. The simple two-or three-letter designation with the round lot trade price, however, is the typical ticker transaction report.

As you can see, following the price of your, stock is fairly easy.

But don't let the ease fool you. Even though it's a simple task, it's an important one. Make sure you know what your stock's price is doing. Remember, while your broker wants you to make money in the market and will help you to monitor your stock, the ups and downs of your portfolio are more important to you. Don't depend on your broker to call with every change in price. Keep track of the price yourself. No one cares as strongly about your money as you do.

Well, you've become quite the investor! Here you are buying stock, voting proxies, attending annual meetings, reading the stock tables and the ticker tape. Pretty impressive! But when do you make the money? When do you get the cash in your hand? When you sell! And when do you do that? No one really knows for sure, but let's go on and see if we can get some tips.

CHAPTER NINE

WHEN TO SELL

You've had that Clunker Car Company stock for over a year now. Twice a week you've checked to see what the stock price was doing. Mostly, it's gone up. There were a couple weeks when it dropped down a point, but it always seemed to gain it back and then some. You bought it at $35.00 a share and when you turned on the TV today and watched the ticker tape, you found the stock went up a quarter of a point from the previous day and closed at $41.50 a share. That gives you a total gain of $6.50 per share or a $650 profit for the 100 shares. Of course, that's not even your total gain. Over the past year you received four dividends of $ .45 per share each. That's $45.00 for each dividend or total dividends of $180. So, if you sold your stock at $41.50 per share, you'd have your $650 gain plus your $180 worth of dividends for a total return of $830 less commissions. That's a return on investment of over 23 percent before commissions! You couldn't have gotten that at any bank!

---

*I made a fortune getting
out too soon.*

J.P. Morgan

As you wonder if you should sell the stock, you reach for

the remote control to switch off the TV. But as you do, you hear the announcer say, "The market has dropped over forty points today. Doesn't look good for the bulls."

What is he talking about? If the market dropped forty points, how does that relate to your stock? And what's a bull have to do with the stock market?

BEARS AND BULLS

Long ago, Wall Street adopted two animals as its mascots —the bear and the bull. These mascot animals were chosen because of their different styles of fighting. A bull, when attacking an enemy, has a tendency to lift its opponent with its horns and throw him in the air. Hence, a bull market is one in which stock prices are increasing or are very high. Therefore, if someone is bullish on the market, they expect stock prices to go high, just like the victim of the bull is "high" in the air. If you believe prices will continue to go up, you are bullish on the market.

The bear, on the other hand, is more cautious in its fighting tactics and tries to knock down its opponent. Thus, a bear market means that the stock market prices are declining or are already down, just like the victim of the bear. Therefore, if someone is bearish on the market, they expect prices to go down.

DOW JONES INDUSTRIALS AVERAGE

But how do you know if the market is going up or down? Some stock prices increase, some decrease, and some seem to remain stagnant. How can you determine a direction for the whole stock market? Enter the Dow Jones Industrials Average (DJIA). The DJIA is the oldest stock average in the world. In the 1890s, financial journalist Charles Dow and his partner, Edward Jones, created the DJIA which was to be used as an indicator of the entire stock market. When the DJIA commenced on January 2, 1897, it was comprised of only twelve stocks. Eight additional stocks were added in 1916, and the Average remained a twenty-stock barometer until 1928, when it was increased to its current level of thirty stocks. The stocks currently included in the average are:

Allied Signal	DuPont	Minn. Mining
Alcoa	Eastman Kodak	J.P. Morgan
American Express	Exxon	Philip Morris
AT&T	General Electric	Procter /Gam.
Bethlehem Steel	General Motors	Sears Roebuck
Boeing	Goodyear	Texaco
Caterpillar	IBM	Union Carbide
Chevron	Int'l. Paper	United Technol.
Coca-Cola	McDonald's	Westinghouse
Walt Disney	Merck	Woolworth

Now that you know what the DJIA is, if it drops forty points, what does that mean for an investor of Clunker Car Company? Probably, not a whole lot. When the DJIA moves up and down, it is a reflection of the entire market—not any one stock in particular. The DJIA could drop forty points in one day, while Clunker Car Company's stock could increase two points the same day. But if the DJIA doesn't mean anything for a particular stock price, what good is it?

Because the DJIA consists of such large corporations, many investors believe the average is an excellent indicator of the economy, which in turn affects stock prices. In addition, the theory is that when the DJIA goes up, investors buy; when the DJIA goes down, investors sell, once again, affecting other stocks on the exchanges. Therefore, while the DJIA does not necessarily predict the performance of any specific stock, it helps investors recognize changes in the market, which in turn are reflective of changes in the economy, which cause changes in business conditions.

But the DJIA isn't the only Average that is used as a market indicator. There are three other Averages which are not nearly as popular, but are regularly quoted in the financial news.

TRANSPORTATION AVERAGE

This Average, developed at the end of the nineteenth century, was originally called the Railroad Average because it was comprised of twenty railroad stocks. In 1970, nine of the railroad stocks were replaced by nine stocks that represented other modes of transportation which were more reflective of the transportation industry in the U.S. at that time. In January 1991, the Average was once again altered when Pan Am Airlines was replaced by Roadway Services, Inc., the first non-NYSE-listed stock to be included in any of the Averages. The twenty stocks that currently comprise this Average are as follows:

AMR Corp.	Federal Express
Airborne Freight	Norfolk Southern
Alaska Air	Roadway Services, Inc.
American President	Ryder System
Burlington Northern	Santa Fe Southern Pacific
CSX	Southwest Airlines
Carolina Freight	UAL
Consolidated Freight	Union Pacific
Consolidated Rail	US Air Group
Delta Airlines	XTRA Corp.

UTILITIES AVERAGE

When this Average appeared on the scene in 1929 it was comprised of twenty utilities stocks. In 1938, however, the number of stocks in the Utilities Average was reduced to fifteen, which is the number used today. The following stocks currently comprise this Average:

American Elec./Pow.	Niagara Mohawk Power
Centerior Energy	Pacific Gas & Electric
Columbia Gas	Panhandle Eastern
Commonwealth Ed.	Peoples Energy
Consolidated Ed.	Philadelphia Electric

Consolidated Nat. Gas   Public Service Enterprises
Detroit Edison   SCE
Houston Industries

COMPOSITE AVERAGE

This final Average is simply a composite of the sixty- five stocks that currently make up the Industrials, Transportation, and Utilities Averages.

When these four Averages were first introduced, each was calculated by adding the closing price of each stock in the Average and dividing by the number of stocks that comprised the Average. Over the years, however, this method of calculation has been altered from a simple arithmetic average to what is called the constant divisor method. Under this method of calculation, the stock's closing prices are added and the sum is divided, not by the number of stocks in the Average, but by a form of that number that has been altered for stock splits, stock dividends, and substitutions of stocks represented in each Average. Because of this form of calculation, the Averages no longer represent the dollar cost of an average share of stock. Instead, they are each viewed as an index that is representative of each sector of the market it represents. Therefore, while these four Averages won't tell you how your particular stock fared over a period of time, it will give you trends as to the condition of the economy, and therefore business in general.

But the Dow Jones Averages aren't the only averages

and indexes of the stock market. Averages and indexes abound in the market. This abundance gives the investor the choice of following whatever specific group of stocks he or she desires. The following are just a few of the other averages and indexes in existence.

STANDARD & POOR'S COMPOSITE INDEX OF 500 STOCKS: Created in 1957 by the Standard & Poor's Corporation, this index measures the changes in stock market conditions based on the average performance of 500 stocks relative to the base period of 1941 to 1943. This index is market-value weighted, which means that high-priced stocks have more influence than low- priced stocks. This index is comprised primarily of NYSE-listed companies, but does include a few AMEX and over-the-counter stocks. The 500 stocks included break down as follows: 400 industrials, 60 transportation and utility companies, and 40 financial institutions.

NEW YORK STOCK EXCHANGE COMPOSITE INDEX: This index is also market-value weighted but includes all New York Stock Exchange stocks which are compared to their total market value as of December 31, 1965, with some adjustments made. Another NYSE index is the New York Stock Exchange Telephone Index, which is comprised of the eight common stocks of the companies that made up the predivestiture AT&T. Additional NYSE indexes are the NYSE Industrial, the NYSE Transportation, the NYSE Utility, and the NYSE Financial Index.

AMEX MARKET VALUE INDEX: This index measures

the collective performance of more than 800 issues representing all industry groups traded on the American Stock Exchange.

NASDAQ-OTC PRICE INDEX: Introduced on February 5, 1971, this index is based on the National Association of Securities Dealers Automated Quotations and represents all domestic over-the-counter stocks with just a few exceptions.

VALUE LINE COMPOSITE INDEX: This index is an equally weighted geometric average of approximately 1,700 New York Stock Exchange, American Stock Exchange, and over-the-counter stocks tracked by the Value Line Investment Survey. The index is designed to reflect price changes of typical industrial stocks.

AMEX MAJOR MARKET INDEX: Produced by the American Stock Exchange, but composed of New York Stock Exchange stocks, this index is a price-weighted average of twenty blue chip industrial stocks. It is designed to replicate the Dow Jones Industrials Average in measuring representative performance in the stocks of major industrial corporations. Fifteen of the twenty stocks included in this index are also included in the DJIA.

WILSHIRE 5000 EQUITY INDEX: This index is the broadest of all averages and indexes. It is market-value weighted and represents the value of all NYSE, AMEX, and over-the-counter issues for which quotes are available. Index changes are measured against a base value established on December 31, 1980.

BARRON'S GROUP STOCK AVERAGES: These averages are the simple arithmetic averages of stocks in more than thirty different industrial groupings. The averages have been adjusted for splits and large stock dividends since 1937.

The above are a few of the stock market averages and indexes that are calculated on a regular basis. As you can see, there is an average or an index for practically any group or combination of stocks imaginable. While these and many more are in existence, however, the one you will hear about the most, and will come to follow, is the Dow Jones Industrials Average.

Now, back to the original question: To sell or not to sell. Despite the forty-point drop in the DJIA, Clunker Car Company closed up a quarter of a point at $41.50. Will the stock's price continue to climb or is it ready to head back down? Of course, no one knows the answer to that question. Maybe the real question is why has it gone up 6 1/2 points to begin with? What makes a stock's price increase?

The answer to that question is supply and demand.

Let's see how supply and demand work in an environment other than the stock market.

Last summer's weather was beautiful—sunny, warm, and just the right amount of rain to raise a nice crop of tomatoes. The grocery stores and the vegetable stands all had good supplies of the red, juicy vegetable. Because everyone could get tomatoes, new recipes started showing up in magazines and newspapers, and everyone started buying more and more tomatoes so they could try the new dishes. Articles that extolled the nutritional aspects of tomatoes were published and people ate even more. With everyone scrambling to buy tomatoes, what kind of price do you think the grocery stores and vegetable stands were getting? Probably a pretty good price because everyone wanted tomatoes—the demand was high.

This year, once again, the weather was beautiful and the tomatoes grew big and juicy and plentiful. But right before it was time to harvest them, a medical research association released a study stating that it was found that the acid in tomatoes causes stomach cancer. Suddenly, no one was buying tomatoes. The grocery stores and vegetable stands had plenty of them in stock, but they were rotting on the shelves. What kind of price do you think they were getting for the tomatoes this year? Pretty low. In fact, they probably couldn't even give them away. But why? The supply was exactly the same as last year. The reason is that there was no demand.

So what do tomatoes have to do with the stock market? Let's say Clunker Car Company announces that sales this year were great and the company made more money than they expected. In fact, they made so much money, they were considering raising their dividend. Isn't this the kind of company investors want to own stock in? It sure is! So everybody starts buying the stock. As more and more people buy, they have to pay a higher price to convince someone else to sell it to them. So the more people who want to buy, the higher the price—increased demand. There are only so many shares available (supply), so as more and more people want them (demand), they're willing to pay more for them.

What happens, though, if the company announces that they sold cars that are defective and they have to recall several models at a cost of millions of dollars to the company?

Because of this additional cost, they won't be able to pay a dividend for at least two years. What happens? No one wants the stock. Everybody starts selling, but the only way a buyer can be found is by reducing the price. Therefore, the price goes down. Just like the tomatoes, the supply was the same, but demand changed, forcing the price down.

So, back to what really did happen with the Clunker Car Company's stock. Why did the price go up $6.50 a share? Increased demand. It's as simple as that. The real question is, why did the demand increase? Have there been any public announcements regarding the company that were positive in nature that would make the price go up? Remember those investor relations people? Call them and see what they think. If they've announced good news recently, maybe the stock will continue to go up. Then again, maybe the news was released three weeks ago, the stock went up, and that's as far as it's going. It's impossible to know for sure, but being aware of what is happening with the company can certainly give you a feel for what the stock may do.

But what if, after you bought the stock at $35 a share, it started dropping and was now at $25 a share? Should you sell? Once again you have to look at the company and see what is happening. Maybe you find out that the president of the company quit to retire in the Caribbean and that's why the stock price decreased. You learn that the company's second in charge has been promoted to president. He's stated that he plans to operate the company the same as in the past. So if that's true, there's no reason the stock shouldn't go back up—except that, according to the analysts, people are a little skeptical about the new president's abilities. The analysts believe the stock price will go back up, but probably only to about $30 per share—not back to $35. So, whether the price goes back to $30 like the analysts believe, or if it stays where it is at $25, you've lost money—right? Not necessarily. There's something called averaging down that may save you from this loss. Here's how it works.

You originally purchased 100 shares at $35 per share—an investment of $3,500. The price is now $25 per share. You boldly buy another 100 shares at the current $25 per share price—an additional investment of $2,500. You now own 200 shares at a total investment of $6,000 ($3,500 plus $2,500). The stock then increases to $30 per share. If you sold all your shares, you'd break even (200 shares times $30 per share equals $6,000). So you were able to keep from losing money without the stock's price ever rebounding back to your original $35 purchase price. By buying the additional stock, you simply reduced your average price per share to $30, which is called your break— even point—you don't lose money; you don't make money; you break even.

But what if, when the price went back up to $30, your break-even point, you didn't sell your stock? Every time the price of your stock increases now, you're making money on 200 shares of stock instead of 100 shares of stock.

Averaging down is great in theory and it's also great in practice if the stock price cooperates. The reality of the matter is that after you bought your second 100 shares of stock at $25 per share, the price could have dropped even lower. Then you'd be losing money on 200 shares of stock instead of just 100 shares. Averaging down is a usable concept, but an investor should understand the risks before using it.

Luckily, your situation right now is that you bought 100 shares of Clunker Car Company at $35 per share and it's now trading at $41.50 per share. Sell? It's totally up to you. Just like when you bought the stock, you had to look at the company and determine whether it was a good buy or not, you now have to look at the facts to determine if this is the time to sell. Maybe you'll sell, then the price will drop drastically. If so, you've made a good decision. Maybe you'll sell, then the price will go way up. Does that mean you've made a bad decision? Probably not. After all, you made 23% on your investment. How could you call that a bad decision?

Another possible strategy for selling your stock is to place a stop order on it. Right now, the stock is at $41.50, but you think it might go higher so you don't want to sell right now, but you're worried that if the price suddenly drops you'll miss the opportunity to sell it at a good profit. So you simply tell your broker to place what is called a stop order to sell the stock at $41 per share.

A stop order is simply an order placed with the broker to buy or sell a certain stock when its market price hits a certain point.

This way, if the price goes up, you still own the stock. If it suddenly drops, when it gets to $41 per share, the stop order automatically converts to a market order, and the stock is sold. That way you won't still be holding it when it drops back to $35. This strategy gives you the opportunity to take advantage of any increase in the stock's price without losing the ability of gaining at least a certain amount on the sale.

When using stop orders, however, it's important to be aware of one problem that could arise.

Let's say you place a stop order at $41.00 per share. The stock never goes below $42.00 per share that day and in fact closes at $42.00 per share. Therefore, the stock isn't sold. But after the market closes for the day, the company announces that earnings for the quarter will be lower than expected. Because of the negative news, the stock opens the next morning at $39.00 per share. Because that price is below your stop order of $41.00 per share, your stop order will be activated and you will sell the stock for $39.00—$2.00 below your stop order. Typically, stop orders are executed at the price set forth; however, it's important to be aware of the possibility of selling below your stated price.

A close relative to the stop order is the stop limit order. This strategy works the same way as the stop order, except that in the above scenario, if the stock closed above your stated price and opened below it, you would not have sold the stock with a stop limit order. The use of this strategy eliminates the problem of automatically selling the stock below your set price; however, if the stock's price continues to drop, by using a stop limit order you could miss out on any gain you would have realized.

Obviously, the primary reason to sell stock is because its price has risen and you have a good profit. But there are a couple of other situations that may encourage you to sell or not to sell. First, whenever an executive of a publicly traded company (called an insider) buys or sells stock in his or her own employer, that transaction must be reported to the Securities Exchange Commission (SEC), which is a federal agency created by the Securities Exchange Act of 1934. This agency ensures that the investing public is protected against fraud and is provided full disclosure of information on securities.

When the insider buys or sells shares of stock in his employer, the SEC makes that information public ,and it is listed in the business section of most newspapers.

If you notice that the insiders are selling or buying a lot of shares, it's something you may want to take into consideration in making either a buy or sell decision.

Another possible indicator of buy/sell strategies is what the institutional investors are doing. Institutional investors are companies that buy blocks (10,000 or more shares) of stock for their pension plans, retirement plans, or their own investment portfolio. Because these institutions buy and sell such large amounts of stock, these transactions can have a direct effect on the stock's price in the open market. Information as to institutional investors' activities can be found in some newspapers that primarily report stock market news, such as *Investor's Daily*.

Of course, you know you can never lose by selling if the stock's price is higher than the price you paid for the stock. But what if the price is lower? Would you still have a reason for selling? We already proved that it can be beneficial if you're averaging down. But would there be any other reason to sell at a loss? One other—taxes.

Let's say it's December 1 and you're holding your 100 shares of Clunker Car Company that you bought at $35 per share. Unfortunately, the current price of the stock is $25 per share. Your accountant tells you that if you sell the stock you'll have a loss of $10 a share, or $1,000 total, but when you file your taxes for the year you can write off that loss, thereby reducing the amount of taxes you have to pay. He says that if you really like the stock, you can always buy it back later. He suggests you sell.

But you think the stock has potential and that it's going to not only go back to $35, but probably go to $40 or $45. In fact, you've even read several articles that agreed with your opinion. So you hate to sell the stock and miss the increase in price. You tell your accountant you're not going to sell the stock, and in March the stock zooms up to $40 per share. You sell your 100 shares and receive $4,000 (100 shares times $40 per share). You had initially bought the stock for $35 per share paying $3,500 (100 shares times $35 per share). Therefore, you made $500 on the investment ($4,000 minus $3,500). You pay your 25% taxes on the gain and end up with an after-tax gain of $375.

Let's now look at what would have happened if you had followed your accountant's advice and sold the stock in December. First, you sell the stock in December for $25 per share and take a $1,000 loss on the sale (purchase price of $3,500 minus sales price of $2,500). That $1,000 loss is deductible from your income taxes. If you are in a 25% tax bracket, you just saved $250 on your taxes, thereby reducing your loss to $750.

In January you once again buy 100 shares of Clunker Car Company, which is still trading at $25 per share— a $2,500 investment. When the stock price rises to $40 per share in March, you sell your 100 shares. You receive $4,000 (100 shares times $40 per share). How much did you make? Your cost was $2,500 (100 shares times $25 per share) and you sold the stock for a total of $4,000 (100 shares times $40 per share). You made $1,500 ($4,000 minus $2,500). Once again, you're in a 25% tax bracket. Therefore your taxes are $375 (25% times $1,500), leaving you a profit of $1,125 ($1,500 minus $375). But don't forget that you lost $750 on that initial sale in December

($1,000 loss minus the $250 tax savings). Therefore, your total income is $375 ($1,125 gain minus $750 loss)—the same as in Scenario 1, when you sold the stock in March. Let's look at those two scenarios once more.

✔Scenario 1: Keep the shares and sell them in March

Purchase Price:	$3,500 (100 shares times $35 per share)
Sales Income:	$4,000 (100 shares times $40 per share)
Income Before Tax:	$500 ($4,000 minus $3,500)
Tax:	$125 (25% times $500)
Income After Tax:	$375 ($500 minus $125 tax)

✔Scenario 2: Sell the shares in December; buy them in January; sell them in March

Purchase Price:	$3,500 (100 shares times $35 per share)
Sales Income:	$2,500 (100 shares times $25 per share)
Loss:	$1,000 ($3,500 minus $2,500)
Tax Savings:	$250 (25% tax rate times $1,000)
Actual Loss:	$750 ($1,000 minus $250 tax savings)
Purchase Price:	$2,500 (100 shares times $25 per share)
Sales Income:	$4,000 (100 shares times $40 per share)
Income Before Tax:	$1,500 ($4,000 minus $2,500)
Tax:	$375 (25% times $1,500)
Income After Tax:	$1,125 ($1,500 minus $375)
Actual Gain:	$375 ($1,125 minus $750 loss)

By selling your shares and repurchasing them, your gain was exactly the same. So why would anyone bother to make the additional sale and purchase if the gain remains the same? Because of the tax consequences. In Scenario 1, taxes on the $375 gain are due that year—in Scenario 2, the taxes aren't due until the following year. That means you get to keep your money and invest it one year longer. In addition, depending upon the amount of gain realized in your stock portfolio, you can probably use the loss to offset gains incurred during the same year.

Of course, when using this strategy, there are issues that must be taken into consideration. First, in this example, we didn't account for the commissions you would have paid for these transactions, but in real life you need to determine if the tax consequences outweigh the commission charges. If so, it's a good way to use the loss for taxes and still get the increase in the stock price.

Second, the example's theory that the stock price would increase to $40 was correct.

However, it's important to always, always, always remember that theories are not necessarily correct all the time.

You could have taken a loss in December then bought the stock back in January and if the price had continued downward, you would have continued to lose money. Or, what if before you bought the stock back, it had already increased back to $35 per share, thereby cutting into your profit? Never forget the risk involved.

There's one other important point to keep in mind. In utilizing this strategy, the investor must wait at least thirty days between the time the initial stock is sold and the time the stock is repurchased. If you sold that 100 shares of Clunker Car Company on December 27 then bought 100 shares of Clunker Car Company on January 5, taking a $1,000 loss, when you claimed the loss on your taxes, the IRS would say, "No way!" This is due to what the IRS calls the Wash Sale Rule, which states that at least thirty days must pass before the second half of the transaction can take place.

Therefore, in this example, you wouldn't be able to buy the shares back until January 26—thirty days after selling the shares on December 27.

That's the strategy of selling for a tax loss. There are also other, more complicated ways to deal with this strategy. However, you should always check with your broker or accountant before attempting to complete a complicated transaction, unless you fully understand the process and its ramifications.

So, we've covered reasons to sell stock when the current market price is higher than your original purchase price and reasons to sell stock when the current market price is lower than your original purchase price. The main thing to remember is to sell the stock when you think it's time. Don't become "married" to a stock and feel you shouldn't sell it no matter what; but also don't panic and sell at the slightest indication of trouble. If the company's profits suddenly decrease dramatically, check it out. Are they spending the money to introduce a new product line or to finance expansion, or are they using the money for day-to-day operations? Find out the reason for any change in the company's financial status, and weigh the impact that change will have on the stock price. After you've done your homework, if you think it's time to sell—sell!

Now, let's get back to the current situation. You're holding 100 shares of Clunker Car Company that you bought at $35 per share and it's now selling for $41.50 per share. You decide the best bet is to sell the stock and take your $6.50 per share profit. You authorize the sale and your broker suggests that you immediately reinvest the proceeds into another stock. You explain that you're not ready to invest quite yet—you're looking at a couple stocks but you haven't decided which one you want to buy. But the broker continues to strongly encourage you to reinvest the money immediately. You agree and buy one of the stocks you were considering. Two weeks later the broker calls and says your stock increased by an eighth of a point so you should sell, take your profit, and buy another stock right away.

If you encounter this type of behavior from your broker you may have a broker that practices the art of churning.

Churning is the practice of buying and selling stocks for no purpose other than to generate commissions for the broker. Every time you buy and sell a stock the broker makes money from his commission. If there's an eighth of a point increase in your stock price, chances are you're going to lose money by selling it because the commission charge will outweigh your gain. You'll lose money, but the broker will make money.

Remember, when you sell a stock it never hurts to put that money in a money market fund or a savings account until you're sure about what stock you want to buy next. Don't be pressured into buying and selling. If you think it makes sense to buy or to sell a particular stock because of specific reasons, go ahead. But if it doesn't make sense to you, and the broker can't give you a good reason, don't do it. Remember, your motive in establishing this brokerage account was to make money for you—not for the broker.

Well, you've covered the gamut. You found a broker, opened an account, analyzed companies, bought stock, and sold stock. And, I might say, you did a pretty good job of it! But is that all there is to stock market investing? It is if you want it to be. But if you want to keep going, there's always plenty to learn.

So far, you chose a specific stock of a specific company and bought and sold it. There are, however, different ways you can buy that same company's stock without doing it the way you just did it.

CHAPTER TEN

SPECIAL TYPES OF STOCKS TO BUY

This chapter deals with special types of stocks that investors can buy, such as REITS and Mutual Funds, which give investors the opportunity to purchase pieces of larger investments that they probably couldn't afford if they had to purchase them alone. In addition, the chapter discusses Primes and Scores which are no longer available to investors, but which demonstrate the type of creativity that exists in the U.S. securities industry.

REITS

Not all stocks on the market are household names like Kodak, IBM, or Campbell's Soup. In addition, not all companies whose stocks are on the market do what most people are familiar with like make cameras, computers or soup. One category of stocks that many people are unfamiliar with is REITs (real estate investment trusts).

A REIT is a company that is organized to pool investors' funds for the purchase or financing of real estate. Their formation was first authorized by Congress in 1960. Immediately, investors liked the concept and the popularity of the REIT grew until 1974, when the real estate industry experienced a recession. After a few years of difficulty, however, REITs re-emerged onto the investment scene.

Today, there are three different types of REITs—equity, mortgage, and hybrid. An equity REIT raises money and uses it for the purchase of real estate, such as hotels, shopping centers, and office buildings. The sponsor (the organization that puts together and sells the REIT) then manages, or hires someone to manage, the operations of the real estate. The operational profits and the capital gains realized when the property is sold are divided among the investors. An equity REIT is a good hedge against inflation, as both rents and property values increase during times of inflation.

A mortgage REIT, on the other hand, raises money from investors, then lends the money to others who want to buy real estate. The mortgage REIT is much like a bank in that it makes money from financing fees and interest on the loans it makes. The mortgage REIT owns no real estate.

Bulls make money;
bears make money;
but pigs always lose.

Ray Bradbury
CBS Sunday Morning

The third type of REIT is called the hybrid REIT and is a combination of the equity and mortgage REITs in that it uses a portion of the money raised to purchase real estate, and it lends a portion of the raised money to others who purchase real estate.

So, what are the advantages of purchasing the shares of a REIT?

DIVERSIFICATION: Most investors can't afford to buy a hotel or an office building; nor could they afford to lend out huge sums of money to others for the purchase of real estate. A REIT gives the average investor the opportunity to invest in large pieces of real estate or to participate in real estate financing. It also gives the investor the ability to diversify into several different types of real estate without investing huge sums of money.

LIQUIDITY: This term refers to a person's ability to convert his or her investments to cash. A bank account is liquid because you can go to the bank and, within minutes, get cash. A piece of expensive art, however, is not liquid because it may take months, even years, to sell and convert to cash.

Unlike most real estate, a REIT is liquid because it is a traded stock. Just like shares of a corporation, shares of a REIT can be bought and sold through your broker. If, on the other hand, you owned the actual real estate and needed cash, it could take months to sell the property and get your money. Likewise, an outstanding loan to the owner of real estate can't be called on a moment's notice. With a REIT, however, a quick call to your broker gets your cash to you fairly quickly, just like when you sell any other stock.

SINGLE TAXATION: Current law states that a REIT must derive 75% of its income from rents, dividends, interest, and gains from the sale of real estate properties, and must pay to its investors at least 95% of all income generated. REITs that meet those requirements are exempt from federal taxation at the corporate level. Dividends and capital gains, however, are taxable to the shareholder. Because of this tax-exempt status at the corporate level, more of the profits of a REIT reach the investors than do the profits of a corporation, which are taxed at both the corporate and shareholder level.

PROFESSIONAL MANAGEMENT: Whether investing in an equity, mortgage, or hybrid REIT, the investor has the advantage of professional management. The investor has no responsibility as to the operations of the property or the management of the loans. Those duties are all taken care of by paid professionals.

So far, a REIT sounds pretty good, right? Well, as always, there are also disadvantages that have to be considered.

LACK OF AUTHORITY: With a REIT, professional managers are overseeing the property or monitoring the loan portfolio, but how do you know these people are competent? Just because they are so-called professionals doesn't necessarily mean they always know what they are doing. However, you have no say in hiring the management people. You have no authority in the operations of the real estate or the management of the loan portfolio.

Your investment dollars are solely dependent upon the decisions the sponsors and their representatives make and the job they do. While their salaries come out of your profits, they may unwittingly purchase an office building filled with asbestos that later has to be removed at a huge expense. Or what if they can't find tenants for the building they purchased, or they make bad loans that never get paid back? There go your profits, and short of proving fraud or negligence, there's nothing you can do about it. It's nice not to have the responsibility of management, but loss of control can be a scary prospect.

VOLATILITY: Remember, shares of REITs, just like other stocks, are traded. Just like common stocks, you can buy shares then have the price increase or decrease. Money can be lost just as easily with a REIT as with any other stock.

Before buying shares of a REIT an investor should read the prospectus, annual and quarterly reports, or other literature received from the sponsor of the investment. Check out not only the investment, but also the company that is offering the investment to see if they have a good track record with past offerings. Ask your broker if he or she has any information regarding the investment or its sponsor. (Be aware, however, that many times brokers are awarded vacations or other prizes for selling a certain amount of a particular investment. Therefore, the broker may be pushing a specific investment, not because it's right for you, but to win a vacation.)

Just like any other investment, a REIT can be a money maker or a money loser. Careful selection and regular monitoring can save a loss of investment.

MUTUAL FUNDS

So you want to diversify your stock purchases, you say? But you don't want to invest in those small risky growth companies? You want to invest in the big boys! The blue chips! IBM, General Motors, General Electric, Exxon, McDonald's, Sears! But you say you have only $2,000 to invest? Can't do much diversifying with that, can you? Or can you? Let me introduce you to the Mutual Fund.

A Mutual Fund is an investment company that is formed specifically to pool investors' dollars and invest them in stocks and bonds and other types of investment vehicles. Because Mutual Funds combine your $2,000 with another investor's $5,000 and another investor's $12,000, and on and on, it can afford to purchase the stocks of several different companies, whether they be small, risky companies or big blue chip companies. You, the investor, then have the advantage of owning pieces of several different stocks that you couldn't afford to purchase on your own.

There are two types of Mutual Funds. First, there is the open-end Mutual Fund which continuously accepts new investor deposits and redeems outstanding shares on a continuous basis. The value of these shares is called the net asset value and is calculated by dividing the current market value of all the stocks owned in the fund by the number of shares outstanding. This number is constantly changing, as the price of the stocks held vary in the open market and the number of Mutual Fund shares varies as investors buy in and sell out of the fund.

One very popular type of open-end Mutual Fund is the money market fund.

This fund invests in commercial paper, government securities, bank certificates of deposit, and other highly liquid and safe securities, then pays its investors a corresponding amount of interest on their investment.

Because smaller amounts of money are pooled and then invested as large sums, investors are able to get more interest on their money than if they tried to invest it on their own. Money market funds were launched in the mid-1970s but gained extreme popularity in the 1980s when interest rates and inflation soared. The money market fund offers investors an interest rate that fluctuates with the market, fund families so that investments can be switched from one to another, and check-writing privileges.

The second type of Mutual Fund is the closed-end Mutual Fund which, instead of continuously accepting new investors, it sells only a prescribed number of shares then closes as of a specified date. The shares of a closed-end trust are bought and sold just like a stock.

So, why would a Mutual Fund company be willing to expend its time and energy in combining your money with other investors' funds, then go out and purchase a stock portfolio for you?

The reason, of course, is fees. There are two distinct

types of Mutual Funds when it comes to fees. The first is called a load fund. This Mutual Fund can be purchased directly from your broker who, as with stocks, can give you advice as to which fund best fits your investing strategy and can even make a recommendation as to the fund you should buy. For this service, however, you will be charged a standard commission fee by the brokerage house. In addition to the commission charge, you will be charged a yearly management fee by the Mutual Fund company itself.

The other type of Mutual Fund is called a no-load fund. Because a no-load Mutual Fund is purchased directly from the Mutual Fund company rather than from a broker, there is no commission charge; however, there will also be no advice forthcoming as to which fund is best for you. The representative of the Mutual Fund company will explain each fund he or she has available and will tell you the investing strategy of each, but it will be up to you to decide which one to buy. While you will not be charged a commission when buying a no-load Mutual Fund, you will, however, be charged a yearly management fee by the Mutual Fund company.

You already know that one of the primary advantages of buying a Mutual Fund is the ability to diversify your investments with a minimal amount of cash. When you purchase Mutual Fund shares, you are really purchasing a piece of each stock that is held in the fund's portfolio. So diversification is a big advantage of Mutual Funds. But what other advantages are there?

PROFESSIONAL MANAGEMENT: When you invest your money into a Mutual Fund, you don't have to worry about whether the pool of funds should be used to purchase stock in IBM or Pillsbury. The fund employs professional managers who analyze the market and specific stocks, then determine which stocks to buy, how much of a stock to buy, how long to hold it, and when to sell it.

CHOICE OF INVESTMENT STRATEGY: Most Mutual Fund companies offer several different types of Mutual Funds. If your investment strategy is to buy stocks of companies that are new and emerging, have a lot of growth potential, but are risky and pay no dividends, you can buy an aggressive growth fund. If, instead, your strategy is to buy stock of companies that pay high dividends but don't necessarily have a lot of share price appreciation potential, you may want to buy a growth and income fund. Or maybe you want to buy a Mutual Fund that invests only in the stocks of gold and silver mining companies, or only in the stocks of oil and gas companies, or one that invests only in foreign stocks, or only stocks of companies that are located in a particular geographic location.

Practically whatever your investment strategy, whether aggressive, conservative, or specific to a major industry or location, you can find a Mutual Fund that is tailored to your needs.

When purchasing a Mutual Fund, you can also match the fund's operations policies to your preference. Some funds invest the money raised and stay with the same stocks for years. Others buy and sell stocks several times a year. Read the fund's prospectus before buying to make sure you agree with the way the fund handles its investing process.

EXCHANGE PRIVILEGES: Most Mutual Fund companies offer several different types of funds (called a family of funds). Typically, within certain guidelines, an investor can switch his or her investment from one fund to another. Therefore, if your investment strategy changes, you have the option of easily changing your investment to match it.

ADDITIONAL INVESTMENT: Once you own a Mutual Fund, most will allow you to add to your investment in fairly small increments. If each month you want to invest an additional $50 or $100 into the fund, you can easily do so. If you choose to add to your holdings each month and you invest the same amount of money each month, you are doing what is called dollar cost averaging. The advantage of dollar cost averaging is that you are buying more shares when the price is low and fewer shares when the price is high, thereby making a larger profit per share when the price increases.

DIVIDEND REINVESTMENT: Just like when you own stock, if a dividend is paid, the Mutual Fund offers you the option of having a check sent directly to you or having your dividends reinvested into the fund, making your investment grow.

Those are the prime advantages of owning a Mutual

Fund. Of course, as we know, when there are advantages to a particular investment, there are also disadvantages.

LOSS OF CONTROL: When you invest your money in a Mutual Fund, you no longer make the decision as to which stock to buy. If you're an animal rights activist and believe pharmaceutical companies should not test their drugs on animals, or if you're an environmentalist and think it's an atrocity that oil companies are spilling gallons and gallons of oil into our oceans, when your Mutual Fund buys shares of a pharmaceutical company that tests its drugs on animals or of an oil company that has a habit of spilling oil in the oceans, there's nothing you can do about it, short of getting out of the Mutual Fund and investing your money elsewhere. While you have no control as to what stocks are purchased, the Mutual Fund company will supply you with a list of the stocks that are in the fund, giving you the option of staying in or divesting yourself of the fund if you don't agree with its purchases or investment strategy.

One other point about professional management—just because these people are so-called professionals, doesn't mean they will always make the right decisions.

Even professionals can make bad decisions. Therefore, if you plan to buy more than one Mutual Fund, even though most companies offer several different funds, you might want to spread your purchases among several companies. If you're unlucky enough to choose a Mutual Fund company that has bad management and goes belly-up, you don't want to own three of its funds. Give yourself the advantage by spreading your risk and buying your funds from different companies.

COMPLICATED TAXES: If you purchase 300 shares of a Mutual Fund, hold it a certain amount of time, then sell all 300 shares at once, you probably won't have much difficulty calculating your taxes. If, however, you purchase 300 shares, instruct the company to reinvest your dividends, three months later purchase 50 more shares, two months later purchase another 100 shares, two weeks later sell 50 shares, you could be in for a complicated tax equation. If you plan to keep your account fairly active, it's imperative that you keep excellent records of your purchases, your sales, all prices, and dates. The reason is that in the above example, the IRS will want to know if that 50 shares you sold were shares from your first purchase, your second purchase, or your third purchase because it makes a difference in the amount of your taxable capital gains or losses. In addition, your dividend reinvestment shares were also probably all purchased at different prices, complicating matters even further. The IRS allows different methods of calculating your taxes, such as the first-in, first-out method or the average cost of shares method, but while the IRS offers you choices, it also offers you a very complicated tax code.

The following is an excerpt from IRS Publication 564, entitled "Mutual Fund Distributions."

☛ *If you received, or were considered to have received, capital gain distributions on mutual fund shares that you held for 6 months or less and sold at a loss, report only the part of the loss that is more than the capital gain distribution as a short- term capital loss. The part of the loss that is not more than the capital gain distribution is reported as a long-term capital loss. There is an exception for losses on distributions of shares under a periodic liquidation plan.*

Obviously, not extremely easy to understand. While demonstrating how tax calculations can become a real headache, however, this dissertation is not meant to scare you away from Mutual Funds. It is simply intended to make you understand how important it is to keep accurate and complete records of the transactions completed in your Mutual Fund account.

When purchasing a Mutual Fund it's important that you treat the transaction the same as you would if you were purchasing shares of common stock.

Prior to your purchase you should obtain a copy of the fund's prospectus, most recent reports, and any other literature that is available.

Many times publications such as the *Wall Street Journal, Forbes,* and *Money.* run articles on the performance of Mutual Funds. Read the fund's literature and any outside material you have; analyze the fund's past performance; make sure its investment strategy is in line with yours; and only when you feel comfortable with the viability of any particular fund, should you buy it.

But once you own it, how do you track its progress? Just like with stocks, most major newspapers carry daily Mutual Fund quotes. Each Mutual Fund company is listed in alphabetical order with each of its funds listed below it. After each fund name are three columns—the first is the net asset value (NAV), which is the nominal value of one share of the fund, and the second is the buy price of the fund, which includes the sales charge where applicable. If the buy price column contains an "NL," you are looking at a no-load mutual fund. The third column tells you how much the price of the fund increased or decreased from the previous trading day.

Mutual Funds give the investor one more choice in the world of investments. By weighing the pros and cons, you decide if it fits in with your investment strategy and philosophy. Only you can determine if it's the proper choice for your investment portfolio.

PRIMES AND SCORES

Remember back to Chapter One, when we asked why someone would want to invest in the stock market? The two main reasons were share price appreciation and dividends. But which is more important? Is it better to buy the stock of a company that is growing and pays no dividend, but has great potential for price appreciation; or is it better to buy the stock of a company that pays a good dividend, but whose price will probably remain stable?

There are varying opinions to that question. The more aggressive, risk-taking investor would go for the appreciation, while the more conservative investor would look for the dividend.

But no matter what you're looking for, it seems the securities market can always create an investment that will meet your needs. For instance, several years ago Americus Shareowner Service Corporation addressed the debate of appreciation versus dividends by entering the market and buying quantities of common stock of several blue chip companies. Keeping those shares, the company separated the income portion of the stock from its appreciation potential and issued units called Primes and Scores, which were simply components of the shares they had purchased.

THE PRIME (Prescribed Right to Income and Maximum Equity) was the income-producing portion of the stock. The investor who bought a Prime received all the dividends the company paid each quarter for that share of stock, but received only the stock appreciation up to a preset dollar amount called the termination price (also called strike price) at the termination date.

THE SCORE (Special Claim on Residual Equity) was the appreciation potential portion of the stock. The investor who bought the Score received no dividends, but received all the appreciation above the termination or strike price of the stock as of the termination date. The termination date was typically set five years from the date of issuance of the Prime and Score. Together, the Prime and Score of a stock made up a unit share investment trust (USIT).

The first Primes and Scores came into existence in late 1983 with the offer of American Telephone and Telegraph stock ,when AT&T was undergoing divestiture. Americus Shareowner Service Corporation eventually offered Primes and Scores, which traded on the American Stock Exchange, on the following 27 blue chip stocks.

American Express	GTE
American Home	Hewlett Packard
Amoco	IBM
ARCO	Johnson & Johnson
AT&T	Kodak
Bristol Meyers	Merck
Chevron	Mobil
Coca-Cola	Philip Morris
Dow	Proctor & Gamble
DuPont	Sears
Exxon	Texaco
Ford	Union Pacific
General Electric	Xerox
General Motors	

These Primes and Scores, however, had definitive termination dates and the last one expired in August of 1992. Americus Shareowner Service Corporation has no plans to reissue any new Primes and Scores due to changes in the tax rules that have gone into effect since the original issue of these shares.

Even though the concept of Primes and Scores is no longer valid, it is a good example of the creativity that exists in the U.S. securities industry. Next year, or five or ten years from now, new products will be on the market that will give investors more choices in investing their money. This creativity means that the learning process of an investor is never ending.

CHAPTER ELEVEN

OTHER WAYS TO PARTICIPATE IN THE STOCK MARKET

BUYING ON MARGIN

You've been buying stock every month now for quite a while, and you've built up about $10,000 worth of various stocks in your street name portfolio. But before you had a chance to invest this month's allotment of your stock budget, your car died and the mechanic took almost all of your monthly investment dollars. It's particularly upsetting that it happened this month because you already picked out the stock you wanted to buy. You studied the literature you received from Colorful Camera Company, you analyzed their financial statements, you read everything you could find on the company and its competitors, and you're convinced the stock is going to increase dramatically in the next thirty to sixty days. But now you're going to miss out because your mechanic is having dinner on your investment money. But maybe you don't have to miss out on your investment after all.

Maybe you could buy that stock on margin.

Buying stock on margin means you can borrow money from your broker and use it to buy stock. But before you do, there are a few important aspects of margin buying that you should be aware of.

First, the Federal Reserve Board, under Regulation T, states that you can only borrow up to a maximum of 50% of the value of the stocks you have deposited with the brokerage house. That percentage, however, does change from time to time, depending upon the availability of credit, the level of inflation, and the amount of margin trading that is being done. In fact, the number can be manipulated to such extremes that it was even increased to 100% at one time, which totally eliminated the purchase of stock on margin. In addition to the Federal Reserve Board requirements, there are also minimum maintenance requirements imposed by the National Association of Securities Dealers, the New York Stock Exchange, and by the individual brokerage firms, whose requirements are typically higher than those set by the other organizations.

My family wasn't affected
by the crash of '29.
They went broke in '28.

Gerald Barzan

You should also be aware that while the brokerage house will lend you the money to purchase stock, it will not be free money. You will be charged interest at the ruling rate. In addition, when you purchase shares on margin, the broker will charge you commissions on the full purchase. Any dividends paid on the stock purchased, however, will belong to you on the full amount of the shares.

Let's look at your situation in wanting to buy the stock of Colorful Camera Company. Let's say the current Federal Reserve Board maximum initial margin percentage is 50%. You go to Alright Brokerage Services, where you have your account, and borrow 50% of the value of the stocks you have on deposit with them. Since you have $10,000 worth of stocks in street name at the brokerage house, you could borrow up to $5,000 (50% of $10,000) against your account and use that money to buy Colorful Camera Company stock. In fact, if the market value of the stocks you already own increases, the amount you can borrow will also increase. Such a deal!

Okay, here's the scary part.

As you already know, the price of stock on the open market can go up and it can go down. You have $10,000 worth of stock right now, but tomorrow the market could drop and you could suddenly have only $8,000 worth of stock. If you've already borrowed $5,000 (the 50% maximum) against that $10,000 worth of stock, when the value of your stock drops to $8,000, you're suddenly borrowing 62 1/2% ($5,000 divided by $8,000) against your stock, which is above the maximum 50%. (In reality, the situation is even worse because interest would be accruing on your account, making the size of the loan even larger.) So now what?

Now you get a margin call from your broker. He or she tells you that you're over your margin limit and you have to bring it back to the 50% level. Here are your choices.

1. You can sell however many shares of Colorful Camera Company it takes to equal $1,000, thereby reducing the amount of money borrowed from $5,000 to $4,000, which is 50% of the $8,000 worth of stock you own.

2. You can give the brokerage house enough cash ($1,000) to reduce your loan to $4,000, which would keep your margin account at 50% (of $8,000).

3. You can deposit an additional $2,000 worth of stock with the brokerage house so that the $5,000 is still 50% of the value of the stock being held by your broker.

When faced with these three options, if you don't have extra stock or cash sitting around, you're going to have to sell some of your stock. Hopefully, if this is the case, the price of the stock will be above what you initially paid for it. If not, you'll be forced to sell it anyway, and you'll have to take a loss on it.

When opening a margin account, most brokerage houses have a 50% initial margin requirement. However, once the account is established, that number often drops to a 30% maintenance margin requirement, meaning that you can borrow up to 70% of the value of your stock portfolio. While this maintenance margin requirement gives you the ability to have access to more money to invest, it also adds more risk to your portfolio, making a margin call an even more serious event.

Buying stock on margin gives you the advantage of using leverage, which is the same as debt. It allows you to purchase more stock than you would be able to if you had to pay cash for every transaction. This gives you greater opportunity for profit and loss, making buying stock on margin riskier than buying stock with cash.

While most stocks traded on national securities exchanges and some over-the-counter stocks are marginable, not all stocks can be bought on margin.

Stocks that sell for less than $5.00 per share cannot be bought on margin, nor can they be used as collateral in a margin account. Often shares in a brand new company or an old company that is having serious financial problems are not marginable either.

Buying stock on margin gives you more buying power, but it also presents you with a higher level of risk. Before using the power of margin investing, make sure you understand the power of its pitfalls.

SELLING SHORT

An old friend has invited you to a party, and while you're there trying to drink a soda and lime and balance a plate full of hors d'oeuvres, someone walks up and extends his hand to you. You manage to shake his hand and introduce yourself, and the two of you strike up a conversation. During the course of your discussion you find that he's also interested in stock market investing, and he tells you about a hot tip someone gave him. He tells you that if you buy as many shares as you can afford of Frank's Furniture Farm, you can't go wrong.

Of course, you know better than to listen to a hot tip, but you're kind of curious, so you decide to check out Frank's Furniture Farm.

You call the company and get the annual and quarterly reports, the 10-K, and 10-Q. But when you get the literature and start to analyze the company, you find it has a book value of $1.15 per share, its earnings per share have been decreasing the last five years to its present $.45 per share, the company has twice as much debt as equity, and its price/earnings ratio is 53. In reading the footnotes, you find there's a lawsuit pending against the company by a customer who visited Frank's showroom, sat in a chair that immediately crashed to the floor and broke the customer's back. You look up the stock in the daily newspaper and find it closed yesterday at $24 per share. Wondering why the stock is trading at such a high price, you call the company's Investor Relations Department, and you're told that the price of the stock shot up three weeks ago when Frank announced his retirement. However, she tells you that a press release just went out that morning stating that Frank has changed his mind and has decided to remain in the president's position for another five years.

The first thing you do is thank your lucky stars you didn't listen to this "hot tip" and rush out and buy the stock! Then you wonder why anyone would buy it. There's no way that stock is going up; it can only go down. So you gather up the company reports and throw them in the garbage can.

But wait a minute. Let's retrieve those reports and think about this. If you seriously believe this is a garbage stock and its price can only go down, there may be a way you can take advantage of that.

You could sell the stock short.

Short selling is a concept that was developed by the Eskimos who used to sell polar bear skins to the European fur traders. Because the European fashions, and therefore demand, were constantly changing, sometimes the furs the Eskimos trapped were worth huge amounts of money and at other times they were practically worthless. Realizing there were huge swings in the price of the furs, the Eskimos took advantage when the prices were high by selling not only their current stock of skins to the traders, but also by selling the promise to deliver the next season's kill at the same price. They locked in the high prices on the skins of animals they had not yet even killed. If the demand and price for the furs dropped by the next season, the Eskimos had made a shrewd deal. If the prices went up, the Eskimos lost money.

Selling stock short follows the same line of reasoning the Eskimos and European fur traders used in selling something before you have it.

> *Basically, when you sell a stock short, you're doing the opposite of what you do when you simply buy a stock, wait for the price to increase, and sell it.*

Instead of the first step of the transaction being buying the stock, the first thing you do is sell it.

That's right—sell it even though you don't own it. What you're really doing is borrowing the stock, typically from your broker. The borrowed shares are then used to make settlement with the buying broker, and the proceeds from the transaction are used to secure your loan. At this point, you have sold the shares but you don't own them—you have what is called a short position. Then, at some point you will have to buy the shares to repay the lending broker. Let's see how you'd do shorting Frank's Furniture Farm.

You call your broker and tell him to short 100 shares of Frank's Furniture Farm at $24 a share. This means that you have promised to deliver 100 shares of the stock at $24 per share at some point in the future. Within two weeks the price of the stock drops to $15 per share. That means that you can now purchase the stock for $9 per share less than what you sold it for. You now purchase the stock for $15 per share and cover your short position of $24 per share. You've made $9 per share, or $900 on the 100 shares, less commissions.

Time to look at the flip side.

What if after you sold the 100 shares at $24 per share, Frank once again decided to retire, and it was announced that the president of the most successful furniture company in the nation was going to replace him. Suddenly the stock's price begins to climb and within two weeks it's trading at $36 per share. If, at that point, you covered your short position, you would lose $12 a share, or a total of $1,200, plus commissions.

Of course, you don't have to cover your short position

right away. You could wait and see if the price came down. But what if this new president does a bang-up job and the price keeps going up and up? Theoretically, there's no limit to the amount of money you could lose. What if the price went to $50 per share or $100 per share or $200 per share! Okay, that's unlikely, but you get the point.

Your loss potential is really limitless, while your profit potential is limited, even if the stock's price drops all the way to zero.

It's important to note, too, that when you short a stock you're basically setting up a margin account in which your losses will be weighed against the equity you have in your brokerage account. If the price of your shorted stock increases to a certain level, the brokerage firm could force you to cover your position at a loss. In addition, if the stock you short pays a dividend, you've got another bill to pay. Remember, you borrowed that stock from someone and sold it. The person you sold it to will get the dividend that comes from the company, but the person you borrowed the stock from still owns it and is entitled to the dividend too. Since you're the one who borrowed it, you're the one who pays it.

So what does short selling mean for the marketplace? The New York Stock Exchange, within certain guidelines, reports the total number of shares of stock that have been sold short in the marketplace and not yet repurchased. Many investors view this number as an indicator of future stock market movement because a large short interest means there is buying pressure on the market, as all those stocks must be repurchased at some point in the future.

Therefore, if the short interest number is high, investors may view that as bullish and anticipate an upward trend in the market. Possibly, the size of the market's short position could be a buy/sell signal.

For you, the individual investor, short selling offers the opportunity to make a profit on a stock whose price you believe is heading downward. Therefore, when analyzing stocks and looking for one to buy, keep in mind that if you find a real dog, it may be a candidate for selling short. Of course, it's important to remember that dogs do bite, and in some cases, can even be rabid. Selling short is a great concept, but just like anything else, it must be understood and handled with care.

PUTS, CALLS, AND STRADDLES

Puts, calls, and straddles are another way you can participate in the stock market without directly purchasing stock.

Once again, these methods use the concept of leverage, making their use much riskier than the straightforward buying and selling of stock.

In addition, these strategies are somewhat confusing in their simplest form and can become extremely complicated when used in conjunction with other market techniques. The following are the basic concepts of puts, calls, and straddles. Once again, their use should typically be reserved for the sage investor; however, it certainly doesn't hurt for the beginning investor to be familiar with the terms and their basic concepts.

153

A call is the option to purchase a stock at a set price (strike price) for a set time period (expiration date). When purchasing calls, an investor believes that the price of the stock will go above the strike price of the call. For example, you purchase a Delicious Food Company July 50 call. That gives you the right to purchase 100 shares of Delicious Food Company common stock at $50 per share anytime before the July expiration date. The purchase price of the call, which is called the premium, was $350. Let's say that Delicious Food Company stock increases to $55 per share. That means you could exercise your option and buy 100 shares of the company at $50 per share, then immediately turn around and sell it for $55 per share—a profit of $5 per share, or $500 total. Of course, you then have to subtract out the $350 premium you paid for the call, making your real profit $150. This call would be considered "in-the-money" because it is profitable.

Not a bad deal, but there is one other choice you need to look at. Instead of exercising the option and selling the stock, you could have simply sold the call at the current premium price. The daily changes in the price of premiums are reported in the financial section of most newspapers.

So if you paid a $350 premium for the call when Delicious Food Company's stock was at $50 per share, the call would be worth even more than that when the stock price increased to $55 because the owner of the call could exercise it and make more money. Because the stock price increased, however, the premium also increased—from $350 to $550—a profit of $200.

> *Therefore, you were better off simply selling the call and making a $200 profit rather than exercising it, buying the stock for $5,000, selling it for $5,500 for a $500 profit minus the $350 cost of the call, leaving a profit of only $150.*

Therefore, when dealing with calls, it's important to determine if you would make more profit by exercising the call or by simply selling it.

Now let's look at what happens when you buy a put. A put is the option to sell a stock at a set price (strike price) for a set time period (expiration date). When purchasing puts, an investor believes that the price of the stock will go below the strike price of the put. This time let's buy a Delicious Food Company July 50 put, which means you have the right to sell 100 shares of Delicious Food Company stock at $50 per share before the July expiration date. The premium you paid for the put was $400. The stock price then drops to $45 per share, making the put more valuable and therefore increasing the premium to $600. Here are your choices:

1. You can buy 100 shares of stock on the open market at $45 per share, then immediately exercise your put and sell those shares at $50 per share. You made $500 minus the $400 you paid for the put—a profit of $100.

2. Because the stock price decreased, the put is now worth a premium of $600. Therefore, you can sell the put for $600, making a profit of $200 ($600 sales price minus the $400 you paid for the put). Once again, this put would be considered "in-the-money" because the owner could make a profit from it.

Of course, it's important to understand that in both of the above examples, instead of making a profit you could have had a loss. If the stock price had declined when you were holding a call, or if it had increased when you were holding a put, they would have been considered "out-of-the-money," and you would have lost money. But how much? Only the price of the premium. For example, when you paid $400 for the right to sell 100 shares of Delicious Food Company for $50 per share, if the price of the stock had gone up to $55 and it was close to the expiration date, your put would be worthless. Why would anyone want to sell 100 shares of stock at $50 per share when they can sell it at $55 per share in the open market? Therefore, you would not exercise the put and you also could not sell the put at that point. If the price of the stock doesn't rebound before the put actually expires, you lose the $400 you spent to buy it.

Of course, if the put expires in July and it's only January, you may find someone who would be willing to buy it at a discounted price on the chance that the stock price might still decline before July. Therefore, the value of a put or call that is "out-of-the-money" decreases as the expiration date approaches. Hence, it is called a wasting asset, as its value decreases over time until it is virtually worthless. (Keep in mind that for purposes of simplification, the above examples do not include the commission you will have to pay when you purchase a put or a call from your broker.)

Another strategy involving puts and calls is straddles.

A straddle is the purchase of a put and a call of the same stock, at the same strike price, and with the same expiration date. In buying both a put and a call, if the price of the stock goes down, the put becomes worthless and you lose the price of the premium. However, the call becomes more valuable, giving you the opportunity to exercise it and make money on the stock, or simply sell the call itself at a profit. Of course, if the stock price increases, just the opposite happens—the call becomes worthless, but the put becomes valuable.

If you have an interest in trading puts and calls, you should be aware of the following.

1. The strike price of the stocks that options are written on begins at $7.50 then increases in increments of $2.50 ($7.50, $10.00, $12.50, $15.00, $17.50, etc.) up to $25.00, then the strike price increases in $5.00 increments ($25.00, $30,00, $35.00, etc.).

2. Options are created for three-, six-, and nine month periods. The last day for trading options is the third Friday of the month in which they expire.

3. An option gives the holder the right to buy or sell one hundred shares of the underlying stock. If the investor wants more shares, more options must be written.

4 . Option holders cannot vote the underlying stock or receive dividends.

As stated before, the concept of puts, calls, and straddles can be extremely complicated and confusing. It may be wise for a novice investor to hold off participating in this type of stock market investing until he or she has become seasoned. The use of any type of leverage always increases the potential risk and reward. And it's important that when investing, you never forget risk versus reward. If you believe the potential reward of a particular investment is astronomical, consider the potential risk—you can be sure it's astronomical, too.

CHAPTER TWELVE

THEORIES AND FORMULA INVESTING

THEORIES

No one can accurately predict on a consistent basis which horse will win a horse race. Of course, that doesn't stop gamblers from trying to develop theories that will make them rich at the track.

Likewise, the stock market has its investors who have developed theories they believe will enable them to accurately predict stock market movements. Some of these theories are complicated; some are fairly ludicrous. Below is a listing of some of the complicated and the ludicrous. Believe what you want.

CUSHION THEORY: This theory states that if large numbers of investors are selling a particular stock short, that stock's price will have to rise because those short positions will eventually have to be covered by purchases of the stock. Technical analysts become especially bullish on a stock whose short position is twice as high as the number of shares traded daily, as price increases will force short sellers to cover their positions, which will make the stock's price rise even further.

DOW THEORY: This theory is based on the belief that the Dow Jones Averages are influenced by three different movements all at once. The primary difference among these movements is time. The first movement is an upward or downward trend that may last for years. The second movement is a major decline or strong recovery in the market that lasts from three weeks to three months. The last movement is the day-to-day price fluctuations. According to this theory, a significant trend is not confirmed until both the Dow Jones Industrials Average and the Dow Jones Transportation Average reach new highs or lows. If they don't, the theory states, the market will fall back to its former trading range. While the theory has many proponents, it also has many disbelievers. Whether a proponent or a disbeliever, however, most agree that the Dow Theory is the most complicated and least understood theory of stock market investing.

It's pretty hard to find what
does bring happiness. Poverty
and wealth have both failed.

Kin Hubbard

ELLIOTT WAVE THEORY: Formulated in 1938 by the late Ralph Elliott, this theory is a technical analysis of trends in the Dow Jones Industrials Average. Via a system that counts and measures price changes in the DJIA, the Elliott Wave predicts future trends in the Average. From these trends, the theory states, the next likely broad market movement for most stocks can be determined.

HEMLINE THEORY: This theory claims that the stock market moves in the same direction as the hemline of women's skirts. If fashion has hemlines trending downward, so will the stock market and vice versa. For instance, the short skirts of the 1920s and 1960s were considered bullish signs that stock prices would rise, while the longer skirts of the 1930s and 1940s were considered bearish. Of course, this theory, along with skirt lengths, has definite upper and lower limits.

KONDRATIEFF WAVE THEORY: Soviet economist Nikolai Kondratieff developed this theory in the 1920s. It states that the economies of the Western capitalist world are prone to major up and down supercycles lasting 54 to 60 years. Based on the crash of 1873, he claimed to have, sixty years later, predicted the stock market crash of 1929. Continuing that pattern, another major crash should have occurred by 1990. If alive, would he say the 1987 downturn was that predicted crash?

ODD-LOT THEORY: This theory claims that investors who purchase odd lots (less than 100 shares) typically are not astute investors and have bad timing. Therefore, anyone who trades contrary to heavy odd-lot trading patterns will make a profit. Proponents of this theory believe that heavy odd-lot purchases in a rising market indicate a reversal, while heavy odd-lot selling in a declining market is a signal to buy.

PRESIDENTIAL ELECTION CYCLE THEORY: This theory states that the stock market moves in relation to the four-year Presidential election cycle. According to the theory, stocks will decline soon after the election as the newly elected President takes steps to curb inflation, government spending and deficits. In addition, taxes may be increased and the economy may enter a recessionary period. At mid-point of the four-year cycle, however, stocks will begin and continue to rebound as the President brings the country through the economic recovery that is necessary to his re-election. The cycle then repeats with the election of a new President or the re-election of an incumbent.

RANDOM WALK THEORY: Developed in 1900 by the French mathematician Louis Bachelier, this theory claims that a stock's past price is of no use in forecasting its future price. The reasoning behind the theory is that a stock's price reflects its reaction to information that comes to the marketplace in random fashion. Because of this random input, a stock's next move is no more predictable than where the next step of a drunken man will be.

SUPER BOWL THEORY: According to this theory, the stock market moves according to which football team wins the Super Bowl. If an AFC team wins, the market will be down for the next year. If an NFC team wins, the market will be up for the next year.

The above are only a sprinkling of the theories that exist regarding stock market investing. Remember, these are only theories—not hard and fast rules.

FORMULA INVESTING

Formula investing is simply investing your money based on a specific formula. It is a mechanical means for ensuring regular, cautious investing. Several different formulas exist. Below is a short listing of some of the more popular ones.

CONSTANT DOLLAR PLAN: Also called Dollar Cost Averaging, this is the process of investing a specific amount of money in a specific investment at certain regular time frames. The advantage is that you are buying more shares when the price of the stock is low and fewer shares when the price of the stock is high, thereby making a larger profit per share when the stock's price increases.

CONSTANT RATIO PLAN: This plan works the same as the Constant Dollar Plan, except that fixed dollar amounts are ignored. Instead, you simply invest 50% of your money in stocks and 50% of your money in bonds.

FINANCIAL PYRAMID: This plan spreads your dollars among investments that have varying levels of risk. According to the plan, there are four levels of investment. First, the largest part of your assets are invested in safe, liquid investments that offer a decent return. Second, some of your money is put into stocks and bonds that provide good income and the possibility of long-term growth. Third, a smaller portion of your money is put into

163

speculative investments which could pay back with high returns if they succeed. Fourth, a small amount of money is invested in high-risk ventures that have minimal chance of success but will pay off substantially if they do come through.

VARIABLE RATIO PLAN: This plan is the same as the Constant Ratio Plan except that instead of keeping 50% of your money in stocks and 50% of your money in bonds, the percentage of funds kept in bonds versus stocks varies. For example, if the stock market rises to a particular, pre-determined high level, a certain amount of the stock portfolio is sold and put into bonds. On the other hand, if the stock market falls to a particular, predetermined low level, money is transferred out of the bonds and into the stock market.

The following two formulas don't fall under the category of formula investing, but are quick little formulas you can use to (1) help determine the effectiveness of the return you receive on various investments or (2) help determine what rate of return is required to achieve certain results.

☛RULE OF 72: From this formula you can determine how long it will take to double your investment money at various rates of return. The calculation is easy. Simply divide the number 72 by the rate of return you are receiving on an investment. For instance, if you invest your money in a money market fund that pays 8% per annum, it will take nine years to double your investment if you don't increase or decrease the investment amount itself (72 divided by 8% = 9 years). Your money will double in 9 years simply by virtue of the interest you receive.

Conversely, if you determine that you want to double your money in 9 years but don't know what rate of return you would need to achieve that result, you can reverse the calculation as follows: 72 divided by 9 years = 8%. Therefore, you would need an 8% rate of interest to double your money in 9 years.

☞RULE OF 115: This formula is the same as the Rule of 72, except that it tells you how long it will take for your money to triple instead of double. Let's say you find an investment that pays 10% per annum. Divide 115 by 10% and you'll find that it will take 11.5 years to triple your money at that rate of return.

Again, we can reverse the calculation and find out what rate of return you would need to triple your money in 11.5 years. 115 divided by 11.5 years = 10%. Therefore, you would need a 10% rate of return to triple your investment money in 11.5 years.

> Whether you invest by a formula or by another plan of attack, the key word is caution. Always remember the rule of risk versus reward, and just as important, make sure you understand the transactions you make.

CHAPTER THIRTEEN

INVESTMENT CLUBS

You've certainly come a long way. You now know how to invest your money in the stock market, how to follow the progress of your investments, and how to determine when to sell your stock. You even know different methods of investing, special types of stock you can buy, and various theories and formulas regarding investing.

You can invest on your own with no problem. But maybe it would be fun to get to know other people who are also interested in investing. Maybe you'd enjoy an investment club.

With the Dow Jones Industrials Average hitting new highs and making dramatic plunges during the last few years, the public has become more aware of the stock market and its activity. This awareness has translated into an increased interest in investing. A result of this interest has been a growth in the number of existing investment clubs.

But why would investors want to join an investment club when they can invest on their own?

Before answering that question, let's look at what an investment club is and how it works.

An investment club is a group of about ten to twenty

people who meet usually once a month to pool their money and invest in the stock market. Typically, the legal structure of the club is a partnership. Upon start-up of the group, the members decide how much money they want to invest each month. Then, members take turns researching companies and presenting potential investments to the group at their monthly meetings. After hearing the presentations, the members vote for the investment they prefer. The majority rules and the investment is made. That's the basic concept of an investment club. So why would people join one when they can take their money to a broker and invest it in any stock they want without having to vote on it?

An error doesn't become
a mistake until you
refuse to correct it.

O.A. Battista

One reason is that by joining an investment club the investor has more buying power. If an investment club has twelve members and they each invest $25 per month, they have $300 a month to invest. That gives them a lot more options in choosing a stock than one person with just $25. Of course, they often have even more than the monthly offerings to invest because they may decide to sell a stock and reinvest the proceeds.

The increased buying power an investment club enjoys also creates another advantage in that the club will pay a lower rate per share of brokerage commissions than someone who invests just $25 a month alone. That's because the more that's invested, the lower the commission rate the broker charges.

Another positive aspect of an investment club is that the research required for finding good investments is spread out. With each member investigating a couple companies, the club can cover a lot of ground in a short amount of time, making the burden of research lighter. Plus, by listening to other members, an investor can learn new investment viewpoints.

Those viewpoints are also expressed through the members' diversity of expertise. When investigating a potential purchase, one member may not notice the footnote in the back of the financial statements that talks about the company's change in accounting methods which will affect the next year's earnings, but the club member who is a CPA will. Or a banker may be more aware of the specific problems the banking industry must overcome before it can make strides in the stock market. Or maybe the human resources professional has a better understanding of the pending union problems a company faces.

Another reason to join is that, just like any other type of club, an investment club offers fellowship.

Most clubs typically have refreshments and time to socialize at the end of their monthly meetings. Some even have parties or picnics during the year.

But once a person is a member of an investment club, how does he or she resign? And how are the investments doled out to the resigning member? Typically, when a member leaves a club, he or she is paid out in cash. Of course, that means the club will probably have to sell stock to pay out the resigning member. Therefore, in their bylaws most clubs make sure they are allowed a realistic amount of time to complete the transaction and make the payment. In addition, the bylaws usually state that the resigning member will be responsible for paying the brokerage commission charged for selling the required number of shares of stock for the payout. In some clubs, when a member resigns, instead of paying them out, they replace that person with a new member who simply buys the resigning member's portion of the portfolio.

That's basically how investment clubs work. So, if you're interested, how do you join one? The hardest part is locating one. The clubs don't advertise or register anywhere, so they're difficult to find. And even if you do locate one, most are small and almost always filled to capacity. The easiest way for someone to join an investment club is literally to start one. But it's not as complicated as it may sound—especially if you elicit the assistance of the National Association of Investors Corporation (NAIC).

The NAIC was founded in 1951 as a not-for-profit organization for the purpose of providing new investors with an investment education and of increasing the level of public participation in the stock market.

For a minimal fee, an investment club can join the NAIC. Membership includes a manual with complete instructions for organizing and operating an investment club, a year's subscription to the NAIC magazine *Better Investing*, and assistance with various aspects of choosing stocks and investing.

Of course, the first step to starting a club is to recruit members—probably a fairly easy task. Friends, relatives, and co-workers may have an interest. And they probably have other friends, relatives, and co-workers who would be interested. Typically, the group should be limited to ten to twenty people for ease of operation.

When a sufficient number of interested people have been located, an introductory meeting should be held. At this meeting potential members can meet each other and learn exactly what an investment club is and how it works. It's important that each member understands what would be expected of him or her as a member of the club. Also at this first meeting, the club's investing philosophy and the amount of money to be invested every month by each member should be agreed upon.

In determining an investing philosophy, the NAIC advocates clubs to follow four investing principles.

✔First, take advantage of dollar cost averaging by investing a set amount of money each month, regardless of the condition of the market. By following this practice the club will buy more shares of stock at lower market prices and fewer shares at higher market prices.

✔Second, all dividends and capital gains should be reinvested, thereby compounding your income and making your portfolio grow at a faster pace.

✔The third NAIC recommendation is to buy growth stocks—companies that have strong prospects of growing faster than the industry average.

✔ And finally, diversify the portfolio. Don't put all your funds into auto, pharmaceutical, or retail stocks. By purchasing stocks in a variety of industries, the club's risk is reduced in the event of a turndown in a particular industry.

When the club has set forth its investing philosophy and has at least ten people who have committed to membership, the investment club agreement should be prepared. Typically, investment clubs take the form of a partnership, but with the assistance of the NAIC material and a quick review of the club's situation by an attorney, any club can determine the best form of organization for itself.

Once the club is legally formed, it's time to choose a broker, begin conducting monthly meetings, and start making investments. This is where the NAIC is particularly helpful, as they offer a myriad of useful forms, investing tips, and helpful services. For more information on the NAIC, write to National Association of Investors Corporation, 1515 East Eleven Mile Road, Royal Oak, Michigan 48067, or call them at (313) 543-0612.

There are a lot of reasons to join an investment club—increased purchasing power, lower brokerage commissions, education, and fellowship. But best of all, it's a great opportunity to invest a little and participate in a lot!

CHAPTER FOURTEEN

GETTING A FAIR SHAKE

AVOIDING PROBLEMS

For various reasons, many people no longer trust investment professionals to give them honest and competent advice. They believe these professionals are more interested in earning a big commission than in placing their clients in sound, prudent investments.

Some of this mistrust stems from past stock market crashes that caught both investors and brokers by surprise, thereby dramatically reducing the value of investment portfolios. Part of the mistrust comes from the news stories we hear of brokers and company officials reaping millions of dollars for their own bank accounts through insider trading and downright fraud. But contributing to the mistrust even more is the array of scam artists and crooks who prey on the average investor on a daily basis.

Everyone's heard the stories of someone investing a life savings in a gold mine that didn't really exist, or in a worthless plot of land that was simultaneously sold to eight different people, or in a pyramid scheme that paid early investors with funds collected from later ones until the whole pyramid crumbled because there were no new investors. Of course, the investors always come out empty-handed. With all this going on, how can you invest your money with someone and feel comfortable that it is in good hands and earning a fair return?

First of all, before opening a brokerage account, investigate both the broker and the firm.

The broker must be registered with the National Association of Securities Dealers (NASD).

For a nominal fee, the NASD Public Disclosure Program at P.O. Box 9401, Gaithersburg, MD 20898, will provide you with a report regarding the broker and his or her firm.

In addition, the firm must be registered with the Securities and Exchange Commission (SEC).

A quick letter to the SEC's Freedom of Information Branch, 450 Fifth Street, NW, Mail Stop 2-6, Washington, DC 20549, will get you a list of any federal records of complaint.

Also, a call or a letter to your state securities commission can produce information on any past disciplinary actions against the broker.

*There are more hustlers
in business than on
street corners.*

Anonymous

Ask the broker for references. Of course, you won't be given the name of someone he cheated, but if at least a few people are satisfied with the service they receive, that's a step in the right direction.

The broker should be willing to allow you a free half-hour consultaion before you sign on the dotted line. He or she should ask about your investing strategies and philosophies, how much you want to invest and what types of investments interest you. Before you invest, make sure you feel comfortable with the broker and his mode of operation.

All of this is fine when you're taking your time looking for a broker, but what about the investment advisor who calls you on the phone and wants to sell you the hottest thing around? You wouldn't fall for that, right? Don't be so sure—some pretty sophisticated investors have gotten burned by telephone solicitors. They can be mighty convincing in their pitch as they take advantage of our emotions. Typically, this is how it goes.

The introduction. Here is where you will learn the broker's name and the type of investment being offered. At first, the investment will be generic, such as "a risk-free investment with a 30% return," or "a gold mine that could strike pay dirt and pay back thousands and thousands of dollars." Then you'll be asked, "Wouldn't you like to make 30% on your money or thousands and thousands of dollars?" Could any sane person really respond with a "No" to that question? Of course not! Besides, everyone knows a little greed now and then.

The pitch. Now you'll get the name of the investment and a quick—very quick—overview of how it works. You'll probably hear a lot of numbers and statistics, and some fairly outrageous claims. If you ask any questions, they'll be answered quickly and flippantly. If you ask too many questions, the person may become condescending and ask why you can't understand the simple concept of the investment.

Once again, your emotions are being used with this ploy to embarrass you so you won't question the investment.

The close. Now you're going to find out that it's imperative for you to make a decision on the spot because this great investment is almost sold out. You don't have time to check with your attorney or accountant or spouse. And if you insist on checking with a trusted advisor or a spouse, you'll probably get another condescending line: "Can't you make a decision on your own? You've got to decide. If you don't buy today, you won't have the chance tomorrow."

Of course, this deadline is just another way to get you to jump on the bandwagon and invest immediately. They want to get your money today so they can move to another town tomorrow and start making calls out of a new phone book.

Remember, when dealing with these so-called professionals, if their investment offers low or no risk, extremely high profits, and they impose a deadline as to when you can invest, chances are, you've got a crook on the other end of that line. Your best bet is to hang up. If, however, you choose to listen, before you commit any money to the investment, at least do the following:

1. Request literature regarding the investment and review it thoroughly.

2. If you don't understand it, have your attorney or accountant review it and explain it to you.

3. Check out the person calling and the firm he or she represents.

4. Find out if the investment is liquid, if you will receive monthly statements, how the rate of return is calculated, and how much of your money will be taken for fees and commissions.

If, after these exercises, you feel comfortable with the investment and you give your hard-earned dollars to this person, follow the investment closely. Make sure you receive the reports you were promised and that dividend payments reach you in a timely manner. Keep in touch with the person who sold you the investment just to make sure he or she is still available.

If, at some point, you become suspicious that the investment is a fraud, demand your money back.

Threaten to go to the regulatory agencies if necessary, but don't agree to wait two weeks for your money. In two weeks the company could be closed and operating in another state. If necessary, offer to pick up your check in person or to pay to have it mailed by overnight delivery to you.

Remember, the best defense against a scam artist is common sense. As the old cliche says, if it sounds too good to be true, it probably is. Don't let yourself become involved in something that you'll only regret later.

RESOLVING COMPLAINTS

Not wanting to get burned on an investment, you follow all the advice and check out the broker and check out your investments before you make them, but despite your diligence, you've chosen a brokerage house that goes broke. What protection and what recourse do you have?

First, the protection. In 1970, when the investment community was recovering from a rash of brokerage house failures, Congress set up the Securities Investor Protection Corporation (SIPC). All member firms of every securities exchange, and all member securities dealers, except mutual-fund-only dealers, are members of the SIPC and contribute to it through assessed annual fees. In turn, the SIPC insures individual brokerage accounts up to $500,000 with a $100,000 limit on cash.

So, the first thing that happens if the brokerage house you're dealing with goes broke is that either on its own or with the assistance of the SIPC, the failing firm will immediately transfer your account to another firm.

This is typically done quickly so investors have immediate access to their accounts. If a transfer is not possible because, for some reason, no other firm wants the accounts, the SIPC will then liquidate the firm and pay off the account holders up to the insured amounts. (Some brokerage firms carry their own insurance above and beyond that supplied by the SIPC.) This process, however, could take several months during which the investor would not have access to his or her account. Therefore, the problem investors face is not so much the loss of their account, but the possible freezing of their account. And during the time an account is frozen, any market fluctuation in the price of stocks owned by an investor is not covered by the SIPC. Therefore, if your account is frozen and the price of your stock is headed down, you can't sell. All you can do is wait. Then, when the SIPC finally liquidates the stock, whatever it's selling for at that time is the price you'll get. Chances are, however, that in the event of the bankruptcy of a brokerage house, your account will simply be transferred to another firm with hardly any time delay.

That is the protection all brokerage accounts are afforded by the SIPC, but what recourse do you have if you have a problem with your account?

If you have a problem with your account, the first thing to

do is call your broker, explain the situation and ask that it be remedied. If the problem is a lost certificate or a late dividend check or something of that sort, chances are, the broker will do everything possible to take care of it. One of the primary ways a broker obtains new clients is through referrals; therefore, no broker wants an angry client walking around.

If, however, the broker doesn't help, you should write a letter to the manager of the brokerage firm requesting his or her assistance in resolving the problem. Typically, this will bring action.

Some problems, however, are much more serious than a lost certificate or dividend check. Maybe you put in a buy order for stock on Tuesday and the broker didn't get around to buying it until Thursday after the price had gone up two points. Or maybe the broker bought more shares than you authorized. When bringing such serious allegations against a broker, you may not get remedial action from the broker or the manager. In that case, your next step would be arbitration.

In 1987, the Supreme Court upheld the clause that is found in most brokerage agreements which prohibits customers from suing brokers in court. Instead, the investor and the brokerage house must arbitrate their differences through industry-subsidized groups such as the

National Association of Securities Dealers (NASD).

When filing a complaint, include in your letter to the NASD a full explanation of the problem and, of course, the name and address of the broker and the brokerage firm in question. You should attach to the letter any documents such as monthly statements, confirmations, or correspondence which will help to substantiate your complaint. The NASD will then investigate the complaint by questioning the broker and the management of the firm and will then make a decision as to what disciplinary action is appropriate.

Of course, the best way to handle brokerage problems is to keep them from happening in the first place.

Do your best to find an honest, competent broker who will work with you to develop a portfolio of sound investments that fits your investing strategy. A good relationship with a broker is as important as a good money-making investment. Expend the time and effort it takes to find the best. It will pay off in the long run.

CHAPTER FIFTEEN

SCRIPOPHILY

When you bought that Finnegan's Finer Foods stock, you certainly thought it was a good investment. But somehow, something went awry. The stock's price began sinking, but you stuck in there, confident it would come back. Then you got the bad news. Finnegan's went into bankruptcy, went out of business, paid its debts with what funds it had available, then informed the stockholders that their stock was worthless.

In frustration, you took that old Finnegan's stock certificate and threw it in the bottom of a drawer. But take heart! You may want to dig out that worthless certificate because it may once again be valuable. The reason is scripophily—the hobby of collecting old stock and bond certificates.

There is in the worst of fortune the best of chances for a happy change.

Euripides

Scripophily started in the United States in the 1970s as an aside to stamp and coin collecting and has grown to be a popular hobby and business. In fact, it's become so popular that the number of scripophilists has swollen to several thousand. There are even certificate auctions held in the US and Europe, and a museum devoted strictly to scripophily has been established in New York.

So why would someone pay hundreds, even thousands, of dollars for the bond and stock certificates of defunct companies? Two reasons—the esthetic value and the historical significance.

The esthetic value of a certificate is primarily determined by its ornateness. While some certificates have no vignettes (the picture on the certificate), such as the ones issued in the 1940s by the Tucker Corporation, which created the Tucker automobile, others have elaborate vignettes. For example, the certificates that were once issued by Ringling Bros.-Barnum & Bailey are filled with circus scenes and an abundance of bright colors—certainly suitable for framing!

But the certificates are not only pieces of art. They also have a definite historical value. For instance, the old railroad companies represent the building of this country. The vignettes that adorn these certificates range from landscapes with American Indians riding across the plains to old locomotives pulling the train cars that carried the much-needed supplies to the early pioneers. Other popular industries include mining, steel, shipping, banking, and insurance. Making these certificates even more historically significant are their age and the signatures that are found on them. Some certificates date as far back as the 1600s, and others carry famous signatures, such as Thomas Edison, J.P. Morgan, and Robert Morris, a signer of the Declaration of Independence.

So in this world of scripophily, what makes one certificate more valuable than another?

☞ AGE: Of course, the older the certificate, the more valuable it is. Generally, certificates dated prior to 1900 are more valuable than those dated subsequent to that time. The reasoning behind that statement leads us to the next characteristic.

☞ SUPPLY: If there are thousands of a particular certificate available, it will be worth less than the certificate that is one of a kind or even one of only one hundred printed. That brings us back to the difference between the certificates dated prior to and subsequent to 1900. Companies that went public after 1900 typically tended to be larger, raised more money in their public offerings, and therefore issued more stock. Just like the stock market, it's simple supply and demand.

☞ VIGNETTE: Typically, the more complicated, ornate, and attractive the vignette, the more valuable the certificate. Again, subsequent to 1900, many companies stopped putting vignettes on their stock certificates.

☞ NUMBER OF SHARES: If a certificate represents a large percentage of a company's total equity, that may add to its value. If it was issued for a large number of shares and is dated in the early 1900s or before, and was a trade of a million dollars or more, there's probably someone substantial behind it. Not many people had that much money back then. The certificate may have to do with some spectacular situation which could make it more valuable.

☛ SIGNATURE: Many stock certificates bear the signatures of people who have since become famous, such as John D. Rockefeller, Henry Ford, Cornelius Vanderbilt, or Thomas A. Edison. In addition, some certificates were not only signed by but also issued to notable people, making the piece even more valuable.

☛ OTHER UNUSUAL ASPECTS: There are other additional characteristics that may make a certificate more valuable. For example, if it hasn't been canceled it may be worth more because typically when a certificate is canceled, holes are punched through it or it is in some way destroyed. Another characteristic that may make a certificate more valuable is if it is from a company's initial public offering rather than a second, third, or fourth issue. In addition, a specimen certificate (one that was a printer's sample and was never meant to be issued) is even more unusual, as there are fewer of them. Historically, the certificate speaks for itself. The signature, the company, if it was a takeover or whatever, the financial history of it alone can make it more valuable.

Another twist to collecting is that it's possible to have a certificate be considered a collector's item even if it's from a company that's still in business and still traded on a public exchange. Many times, just as companies change their packaging designs or logos, they change their certificates. An original certificate from an older company that now has a new certificate design may not only be valuable from a per share perspective, but possibly also from a collector's standpoint. For instance, for years the Playboy Enterprises stock certificate was adorned with the nude picture of Willy Rey, Miss February 1971. In June 1990, the company changed the vignette to a woman dressed in a flowing robe, holding a globe, to depict the company's international aspirations. Those original certificates are now collectors items.

Another part of the fun of collecting is the research that can be done on these certificates. Who signed it? Who was it issued to? What's the story behind the company?

But will these certificates continue to increase in value? They certainly have during the past several years and with the number of collectors rapidly increasing, supply and demand will dictate higher prices. In fact, prices have already increased to the point that in 1990, a certificate signed by Frederic the Great's father sold for $62,000.

Another factor that may cause certificates to continue to increase in value is the current push in the securities industry to eliminate stock certificates altogether, which would, of course, reduce the supply coming into the market.

So, if you decide to take up the hobby of scripophily, where should you begin? The main thing is to start small. Buy a couple certificates, research them, and figure out what makes them valuable.

Whether a certificate turns out to be a real find and extremely valuable or just a conversation piece, scripophily can be an interesting hobby. Stock market investors who find it stressful to watch stock prices soar, then dive, or who don't like dealing with stockbrokers, may find comfort in purchasing certificates purely for their esthetic and historical value. While the beauty of a stock's price increasing threefold is invigorating, the opportunity of holding a certificate that's 200 years old and signed by one of our famous ancestors can be just as thrilling.

CHAPTER SIXTEEN

THE STOCK MARKET OF THE FUTURE

Just like anything else in this world, the stock market keeps changing. Being a broker is no longer a side job for a waiter in a restaurant; the American Stock Exchange no longer conducts its trading at curbside; and investors' accounts are no longer uninsured in the event of a brokerage firm failure.

Today's stock market is modern, computerized, fast-paced, and streamlined. What changes could we possibly see that would enhance its efficiency further?

First of all, many people believe that in the near future stock certificates will no longer exist. Instead, trades will be recorded through an entry into a computer, and an investor's only physical proof of ownership will be his or her monthly statement.

Another possible change is that brokerage houses will no longer accept checks for settlement on purchases.

Instead, all purchases will be made with automated funds, or an investor will have to maintain a cash account with his or her brokerage house so that funds can be quickly verified and transferred. Of course, this would be great for the brokerage houses, as many investors who now keep their cash separate from their brokerage accounts would move their funds to the brokerage firms, increasing the firms' business tremendously.

If changes are made so that future trades are indeed paid for with automated funds, and the issuance of stock certificates is eliminated, the brokerage community would then be able to reduce the current five-day settlement period, streamlining the trading process even further. There is a fear, however, that some investors would be unwilling to maintain the required cash accounts or accept a computerized form of ownership and would, therefore, be driven from the market.

In addition to stock certificates, dividend checks could also be a thing of the past. In the future, companies may automatically deposit their investors' dividends directly into their savings or checking accounts.

Of course, a result of these changes could be that the smaller, regional brokerage firms would not be able to afford the computer hardware and software it takes to conform to these modifications. Therefore, they could possibly be forced to close their doors or sell out to the big houses, leaving only gigantic firms with whom to do business.

A more global approach to investing is also a strong possibility for the future. Settlement periods and other administrative aspects of the stock markets of countries worldwide may be standardized so that investments can be made more freely between foreign exchanges, forming a global market.

You can also be sure that new types of investments and new ways of investing will enter the marketplace, creating an even wider array of investment choices.

As the world changes, so too will the stock market. With improved communication systems and a heavier reliance on computerization, investing will become more stream-lined and faster paced. An investor's choice of investments will increase as will the complexity of the investments offered. Trading hours on the public exchanges could be expanded to give investors the ability to make trades possibly even twenty-four hours a day.

It's pretty hard to find what
does bring happiness. Poverty
and wealth have both failed.
Kin Hubbard

But no matter how complex and how fast paced the world of investing becomes, the same old rules apply. Don't invest in something you don't understand; don't let anyone convince you to invest on the spur of the moment without the chance to review the investment; be sure to follow your investment portfolio closely; and most importantly, remember the concept of risk versus reward. With those rules in mind, you'll enjoy the challenge and the excitement the stock market offers. This is your chance to be in control of your financial future.

May you always buy low and sell high!

> *Those who condemn wealth are
> those who have none and see
> no chance of getting it.*
>
> <u>William Penn Patrick</u>

GLOSSARY

AMERICAN STOCK EXCHANGE (AMEX): Second largest stock exchange in the US Originally called the Curb Exchange, as it originated as an outdoor market located near Wall Street, where trading took place in the street.

ANALYST: Brokerage firm employee whose job is to research and analyze companies' stocks to determine if a certain stock is best to be bought or sold at a specific point in time.

ANALYST REPORT: Report issued by a brokerage firm analyst. The analyst reports are made available to the firm's clients.

ANNUAL MEETING: Once-a-year meeting of a public company's shareholders. Management presents an overview of the company's past year and discusses future plans. Shareholders are requested to vote on certain issues affecting the company.

ANNUAL REPORT: Booklet put together by a public company each year to communicate to the investment community the company's operations for the past year. Typically consists of at least four sections: Letter to Shareholders, Review of Operations, Audited Financial Statements, and Consolidated Footnotes.

ASKED PRICE: The price an investor must pay to purchase a stock.

ASSETS: Anything a company owns. All of a company's assets are listed on its balance sheet.

AUDITOR'S OPINION: The section of a company's annual financial statements in which the auditors give their opinion as to whether they agree that the statements present fairly the financial position of the company and if the results of its operations are in conformity with generally accepted accounting principles.

AUTHORIZED STOCK: Stock legally created by a company in anticipation of a public offering.

AVERAGING DOWN: Purchasing additional stock of a company whose stock price has decreased, subsequent to your initial purchase, in order to reduce the average price of your stock holdings in the company.

BALANCE SHEET: A financial statement that looks at a company's financial status at a specific point in time, usually the last day of a quarter or fiscal year.

BEAR MARKET: A market in which stock prices are declining or are already low.

BID PRICE: The price an investor will receive when selling a stock.

BLOCK: A large amount of stock (typically 10,000 shares or more) sold as a single unit.

BLUE CHIP STOCKS: Stocks that are considered to be of the highest quality and not very risky. Stocks of stable, long-established companies that are leaders in their industry, that have a history of good earnings growth and of paying regular dividends.

BOOK VALUE: The closest actual value that can be placed on a stock. It is calculated by dividing the company's shareholders' equity (net worth) by the number of shares outstanding. Book value is how many dollars worth of equity the company has for every share of stock sold.

BREAK EVEN POINT: The point when a stock's price is at the level where you don't lose money, you don't make money, you break even.

BULL MARKET: A market in which stock prices are increasing or are already very high.

CALL: An option to purchase a stock at a set price (strike price) for a set time period (expiration date).

CAPITAL GAIN: The profit realized when an investment is sold for more than its purchase price.

CAPITAL LOSS: The amount of money lost when an investment is sold for less than its purchase price.

CASH DIVIDEND OPTION: An investor's option of receiving his or her dividend in check form each dividend-paying period. The checks can be sent directly to the investor, or the investor can arrange to have them sent to a bank account or brokerage account.

CASH FLOW STATEMENT: See Statement of Changes in Financial Position.

CASH OPTION PROGRAM: Program offered by many companies in which current shareholders, who are participating in the company's dividend reinvestment program, can mail in additional cash contributions each quarter so the company can purchase additional shares of stock in the investor's name.

CERTIFICATE: A negotiable instrument that evidences ownership of stock in a particular company.

CHURNING: The practice of buying and selling stocks for no purpose other than to generate commissions for the broker.

CLOSELY HELD CORPORATION: A company that raises money by selling stock, but only to a very limited number of individuals. Typically, the stock of a closely held corporation is not traded on an exchange.

COMMISSION: The stockbroker's fee for completing stock transactions for a customer. The amount of fees charged vary widely between full-service brokers and discount brokers, depending on the level of service offered by each.

COMMON STOCK: A unit of ownership in a public company. It is the first type of stock to be issued and the riskiest type of stock to purchase.

COMMUNITY PROPERTY: Property that is owned jointly by a husband and wife by fact of their marriage. State laws vary on the applicability of community property.

COMPOSITE AVERAGE: A mathematical calculation consisting of the current price of each of the sixty-five stocks that make up the Industrials, Transportation, and Utilities Averages.

CONFIRMATION: A statement confirming the transaction between a brokerage firm and its client for the purchase or sale of securities.

CONSTANT DIVISOR METHOD: Method of calculating the four Dow Jones Averages. The stocks' closing prices are added and the sum is divided, not by the number of stocks in the Average, but by a form of that number that has been altered for stock splits, stock dividends, and substitutions of stocks represented in each Average.

CONVERTIBLE STOCK: Preferred stocks which can be converted to common stock at some future date.

CORPORATE BOND: A negotiable security a company sells to raise money through debt.

CUMULATIVE PREFERRED STOCK: A preferred stock which accumulates any dividends that, for some reason, were not paid in previous years. If a cumulative preferred stock dividend is not paid in one year, those shareholders will receive two dividends the following year before the common shareholders receive any dividend.

CURB EXCHANGE: Now known as the American Stock Exchange, it was initially called the Curb Exchange because it originated as an outdoor market located near Wall Street, where trading took place in the street.

CURRENT ASSETS: Any assets a company will convert to cash within one year.

CURRENT LIABILITIES: Any liabilities a company must pay within one year.

CURRENT RATIO: This ratio determines how many times a company's current liabilities could be paid with its current assets. It is calculated by dividing the current assets by the current liabilities.

CUSTODIAN ACCOUNT: An account in which the actual owner turns over control of the account to someone else— the custodian. Typically used for minors and IRA accounts.

DEBT: A method of raising money used by companies instead of selling stock. By using debt, the company borrows money from an institutional lender or sells bonds, thus retaining full ownership of the company and remaining private.

DEBT-TO-EQUITY RATIO: Comparison of a company's long-term debt or total debt to its shareholders' equity. It is a measure of leverage. Calculated by dividing either long-term or total debt by shareholders' equity.

DECLARATION DATE: The day a company announces how much per share it will pay in dividends for that specific period.

DILUTION: The "watering down" of stock by adding shares to those already issued and outstanding. While there are more shares in the marketplace, each share is worth less than it was before the additional shares were sold.

DISCOUNT BROKERAGE FIRM: Brokerage firm that is strictly in the business of placing buy and sell orders for clients. Does not give advice or recommendations, however, offers lower commission charges.

DISCRETIONARY ACCOUNT: The type of brokerage

account in which the investor gives power of attorney to the broker to make buy and sell decisions.

DIVERSIFY: To include in one's stock portfolio the stocks of companies that are involved in various industries so that the investor's exposure to a downturn in one industry is not so great.

DIVIDEND: The portion of a company's profits that the Board of Directors decides to pay to the shareholders. Typically, dividends are paid quarterly.

DIVIDEND REINVESTMENT OPTION: An investor's option of having his or her dividend used to purchase additional shares of the company's stock in the investor's name. The purchases are sometimes made with no commission charge or at a discounted price.

DOW JONES INDUSTRIALS AVERAGE (DJIA): A mathematical calculation consisting of the current price of thirty blue chip stocks that are traded on the New York Stock Exchange. This index is used as an indicator for the whole US stock market system.

EARNINGS PER SHARE (EPS): A measure of how much money a company made during the year on a per-share basis. Calculated by dividing net earnings by the number of shares issued and outstanding.

EQUITY: Stocks that carry risk and share in profits through dividends. When a company raises money through equity, it does an initial public offering by issuing and selling stock.

EX-DIVIDEND DATE: The first day on which someone purchasing a company's stock would not receive the most recently-announced dividend. Typically, the stock price will move up by the amount of the dividend prior to the ex-dividend date, then fall by the same amount after the ex-dividend date.

EXCHANGE: An institution that provides the facilities for trading securities. The exchange does not buy or sell stock, nor does it set any prices.

EXPENSES: The amount of money a company spends to operate.

EXTRAORDINARY ITEM: Expense or income item that is neither a part of the normal running of a business nor occurs every year.

FAMILY OF FUNDS: Grouping of different types of mutual funds offered by one company. Typically, an investor can switch his or her investment from fund to fund.

FINANCIAL STATEMENTS: Accounting statements issued by a public company that depict the company's current status and past operations. The three primary statements are the balance sheet, the income statement, and the statement of changes in financial position.

FISCAL YEAR: Twelve-month period for which the company prepares its financial statements. Fiscal years often coincide with the calendar year, however, many companies end their fiscal year during other months.

FOOTNOTES: Typically the last section of the annual report, the footnotes support and explain the information that is found in the financial statements.

FORMULA INVESTING: The process of investing money based on a specific formula. It is a mechanical means for ensuring regular, cautious investing.

FREE-RIDING: An illegal practice by investors of purchasing stock, but not paying for it. If the stock price increases, the investor sells and pays the broker, making a profit. If the stock price decreases, the investor vanishes, or argues that the order to buy was never issued.

FULL-SERVICE BROKERAGE FIRM: A brokerage firm that not only fills buy and sell orders, but also gives advice and stock recommendations to its clients. In order to provide this additional service, a higher commission rate is charged.

FUNDAMENTAL ANALYSIS: Predicting the future movements of a stock based on an analysis of the company's financial statements.

GROWTH STOCKS: Typically, stocks of companies that are young and fast-growing or in volatile industries. These stocks do not usually pay dividends but they offer good potential for stock price appreciation.

HOLDER OF RECORD: The investor whose name appears in a company's shareholder records.

IN-THE-MONEY: If an investor's call option exercise price is below the price of the underlying stock, the call is said to be in-the-money. For a put to be in-the-money, the put option exercise price would have to be above the price of the underlying stock.

INCOME: The amount of money or revenues received by a company.

INCOME STATEMENT: A financial statement that describes how well the company performed during a specific period of time—usually for one year or three months. It shows income, expenses, and profit.

INCOME STOCKS: The stocks of established, stable companies in mature industries. These companies have a history of paying a steady dividend stream.

INDIVIDUAL ACCOUNT: An account in which there is only one owner. In the event of the owner's death, the stock becomes part of the estate; therefore, it can be bequeathed in the owner's will to whomever he or she desires.

INITIAL PUBLIC OFFERING (IPO): The process through which a company legally creates stock and sells it to the public (through a brokerage firm) for the first time.

INSIDER: The employee of a publicly-traded company who has access to information which could affect the price of the company's stock.

INSTITUTIONAL INVESTOR: Companies that buy blocks of stock for their pension plans, retirement plans, or their own investment portfolio.

INVESTMENT CLUB: A group of ten to twenty people who meet, usually once a month, to pool their funds and make joint investment decisions.

INVESTOR RELATIONS DEPARTMENT: Group of employees whose function is to act as a liaison between the company and the investment community.

ISSUED AND OUTSTANDING STOCK: The portion of authorized stock that is sold to the public.

JOINT TENANTS WITH RIGHT OF SURVIVORSHIP (JT WROS): A type of ownership in which each person listed on the account owns an equal share of all securities purchased. If one joint tenant dies, his or her portion of the portfolio automatically becomes the property of the surviving joint tenant(s).

LETTER TO SHAREHOLDERS: The letter contained in a company's annual or quarterly report that discusses the company and its performance during the past year or quarter. Typically, the letter is signed by the chairman and/or president of the company.

LEVERAGE: The relationship between a company's borrowed funds and its shareholders' equity.

LIABILITIES: Anything a company owes. All of its liabilities are listed on its balance sheet.

LIMIT ORDER: A buy order issued to a broker from his or her client that designates a specific price at which the stock must be purchased.

LONG-TERM DEBT: Debts that are not due to be paid for at least one year.

LOSS PER SHARE: A measure of how much money a company lost during the year on a per-share basis. Calculated by dividing the net loss by the number of shares issued and outstanding.

MARGIN ACCOUNT: An account that allows an investor to borrow money from the stockbroker to buy stocks. Regulation T of the Federal Reserve Board regulates the use of margin accounts.

MARGIN CALL: The request from the broker for additional funds when an investor's margin account does not maintain the proper balance between funds borrowed and stocks used as collateral. The investor can remedy the situation by selling stock, infusing cash into his or her account, or offering additional stock for collateral.

MARKET ORDER: A buy order in which the broker can purchase the stock at the next available price on the exchange.

MONEY MARKET FUND: An open-end mutual fund that invests in highly liquid, safe securities, then pays its investors a corresponding amount of interest on their investment. Because smaller amounts of money are pooled and invested as large sums, investors typically get a higher rate of interest on their money. The money market fund offers investors an interest rate that fluctuates with the market, fund families, and check-writing privileges.

MUTUAL FUND: An investment company that is formed specifically to pool investors' dollars and invest them in stocks, bonds and other types of investment vehicles. The two types of mutual funds are (1) open-end, which continuously accepts new investor deposits and redeems outstanding shares on a continuous basis, and (2) closed-end ,which sells only a prescribed number of shares then closes as of a specified date. Also, load funds are sold through a broker, and therefore a commission fee is charged, whereas no-load funds are purchased directly from the mutual fund company and no commission fee is charged. Investors in either type of fund will be charged yearly management fees and possibly other additional fees.

NATIONAL ASSOCIATION OF INVESTORS COR-PORATION (NAIC): Founded in 1951, a not-for-profit organization formed for the purpose of providing new investors with an investment education and of increasing the level of public participation in the stock market. The NAIC, for a minimal membership fee, offers advice and assistance in organizing and operating investment clubs.

NATIONAL ASSOCIATION OF SECURITIES DEALERS AUTOMATED QUOTATION (NASDAQ): A computerized stock trading system that provides up-to-date information on stocks traded in the over-the-counter market.

NET ASSET VALUE: The actual value of shares in a mutual fund. Calculated by dividing the current value of all stocks owned in the fund by the number of shares out-standing.

NET INCOME: The amount of money a company makes during a specific period of time. It is calculated by subtract-ing all of the company's expenses from its total income.

NET LOSS: The amount of money a company loses during a specific period of time. If total expenses are higher than total income, the result is a net loss instead of net income.

NET WORTH: The amount of money the investors have

put into a company plus earnings that have been kept in the company instead of being paid out in dividends. Same as shareholders' equity.

NEW YORK STOCK EXCHANGE (NYSE): Also called the Big Board, it is the largest US exchange, transacting 85% to 90% of the total volume of business in listed securities.

NO-RISK INVESTMENT: Misnomer. No such thing exists.

ODD LOT: A number of shares of stock that is less than a round lot (100 shares). Typically, investors dealing in odd lots are charged premium brokerage rates due to the administrative hassle of odd lots.

OUT-OF-THE-MONEY: If an investor's call option exercise price is above the price of the underlying stock, the call is said to be out-of-the-money. For a put to be out-of-the-money, the put option exercise price would have to be below the price of the underlying stock.

OVER THE COUNTER (OTC): A telephone/computer market to which stockbrokers subscribe in order to communicate bids and offers on stocks to each other.

PAPER LOSS: The difference between what an investor paid for shares of stock and the decreased current market value of that stock. As long as the stock is not sold, the loss is only on paper and not actual.

PAPER PROFIT: The difference between what an investor paid for shares of stock and the increased current market value of that stock. As long as the stock is not sold, the profit is only on paper and not actual.

PAY DATE: The date a company puts the dividend checks in the mail to the investors or credits the investors' accounts with their dividend reinvestment shares. It is the date on which the dividend must be paid.

PENNY STOCKS: Stocks that are very low priced. Considered to be fairly risky.

POINT: Same as a dollar. If the price of a share of stock went up one point, it went up one dollar.

PORTFOLIO: A person's stock and/or other financial instrument investments.

PREFERRED STOCK: Stock a company may issue subsequent to issuing common stock. Investors who purchase preferred stock do not have voting rights, but have a set dividend that is more secure than that of the common shareholders. In addition, in the event of the liquidation of the company, the preferred shareholders would receive their money prior to the common shareholders receiving theirs.

PREMIUM: The price an investor must pay to purchase a put or a call.

PRICE/EARNINGS RATIO (P/E): A ratio that tells how many times a company's earnings per share a stock is selling for in the marketplace. It is calculated by dividing the price of one share of the company's stock by its annual earnings per share, which is found on the income statement.

PRIMARY MARKET: The market for stocks when they are first sold to the public when a company does an initial public offering in order to raise money. The sale of these stocks in the primary market is handled through stockbrokers.

PRIME: Acronym for Prescribed Right to Income and Maximum Equity. When a share of stock is divided into a Prime and a Score, the Prime is the part of the stock that is considered income-producing, as it receives the full dividend but only a preset portion of any share price appreciation.

PRIVATE COMPANY: A company that has not issued stock to raise money and therefore has not sold part of its equity. When a private company needs to raise money, it does so through debt by either borrowing from a lending institution or selling bonds.

PROXY: An invitation to a company's shareholders to attend the annual meeting. The proxy explains what issues will be brought to a shareholder vote.

PROXY CARD: The card included with a proxy that

shareholders can use to cast their vote prior to the annual meeting.

PUBLIC COMPANY: A company that, through an initial public offering, legally created and sold stock in order to raise money and therefore sell part of its equity to shareholders. A public company has certain reporting obligations to its shareholders, which are policed by the Securities and Exchange Commission.

PUT: An option to sell a stock at a set price (strike price) for a set time period (expiration date).

QUARTERLY REPORT: A report prepared by a public company that is used to communicate to the investment community what has happened at the company during a specific three-month period.

RAILROAD AVERAGE: Developed at the end of the nineteenth century, it was an average of the prices of twenty railroad stocks that was to be used as a barometer of the transportation industry. In 1970, nine of those railroad stocks were replaced with stocks of other types of transportation companies to reflect the changing industry. The method of calculation has also since been altered. Currently known as the Transportation Average.

REAL ESTATE INVESTMENT TRUST (REIT): A company that is organized to pool investors' funds for the purchase or financing of real estate. An equity REIT uses the money raised to purchase real estate; a mortgage

REIT uses the money raised to finance others buying real estate; and a hybrid REIT is a combination of the two.

REAL LOSS: The difference between what an investor paid for shares of stock and the decreased amount received when those shares are sold. Any brokerage commissions paid increase a real loss.

REAL PROFIT: The difference between what an investor paid for shares of stock and the increased amount received when those shares are sold. Any brokerage commissions paid decrease a real profit.

RECORD DATE: The date when the books of a company are closed. The shareholders recorded in the books as of the close of that day will receive the dividend for that period.

REGISTERED ACCOUNT: A brokerage account in which the investor's name is listed as the owner, making the investor responsible for the handling and safekeeping of the stock certificate.

RETURN ON EQUITY: A ratio that shows what percent return a company is realizing on its net worth. It is calculated by dividing net earnings by shareholders' equity.

REVERSE STOCK SPLIT: A decrease in the number of shares issued by a company without any change in its financial position. Companies typically do a reverse stock split when their stock price is so low that most investors pass it over because it is so cheap. A ten-for-one reverse stock split would increase the price of a $1 stock to $10.

REVIEW OF OPERATIONS: A section of a company's annual report that describes the company's products and markets and explains exactly what the company manufactures or sells or what services it offers. This section should not only contain a discussion of what the company did during the past year, but also a discussion of its plans for the future.

RISK VERSUS REWARD: The relationship between the amount of potential risk in an investment and the amount of potential reward in the same investment. Typically, the riskier the investment, the higher the reward and vice versa.

ROUND LOT: An even one hundred shares. Anything less is typically considered an odd lot.

ROUND TRIP DISCOUNT: The offer of an additional discount on brokerage fees if the investor buys and sells a stock through the same brokerage firm within a certain time frame—usually sixty days.

RULE 405: An ethical concept set forth by the NYSE stating that all brokers must "know their clients," because an investment that is suitable for one client may not be appropriate for another.

RULE OF 72: A formula for determining how long it would

take to double the dollar amount of an investment that is earning a specific rate of return. Conversely, can be used to determine what rate of return an investment must earn to double the dollar amount in a specified number of years.

RULE OF 115: A formula for determining how long it would take to triple the dollar amount of an investment that is earning a specific rate of return. Conversely, can be used to determine what rate of return an investment must earn to triple the dollar amount in a specified number of years.

SCORE: Acronym for Special Claim on Residual Equity. When a share of stock is divided into a Prime and a Score, the Score is considered the appreciation potential portion of the stock as it receives no dividend, but receives all appreciation above the termination or strike price of the stock as of the termination date.

SCRIPOPHILY: The hobby of collecting old stock and bond certificates. Started in the US in the 1970s as an aside to coin and stamp collecting.

SEAT: Term that denotes membership in a stock exchange. A person must be a member to trade stocks. The cost of a seat continually changes.

SECONDARY MARKET: Any trading of a company's stock between investors subsequent to the initial public offering. The company receives no money from these transactions.

SECURITIES AND EXCHANGE COMMISSION (SEC): A federal agency created by the Securities Exchange Act of 1934. The agency ensures that the investing public is protected against fraud and provided full disclosure of information on securities.

SECURITIES INVESTOR PROTECTION CORPORATION (SIPC): Set up by Congress in 1970, the SIPC insures individual brokerage accounts up to $500,000 with a $100,000 limit on cash. All brokers and dealers registered with the SEC and with national stock exchanges must become members and contribute through assessed annual fees.

SECURITY: Any marketable financial instrument including not only stocks, but also bonds, mutual funds, and debentures.

SETTLEMENT DATE: The date on which an investor purchasing stock actually becomes the owner or the date on which an investor selling stock is officially no longer the owner. The settlement date is always five business days after the trade date. The investor must settle his or her account during those five days.

SHARE PRICE APPRECIATION: An increase in the price of a share of stock after it is purchased.

SHARE PRICE DEPRECIATION: A decrease in the price of a share of stock after it is purchased.

SHAREHOLDER'S EQUITY: The amount of money investors have put into the company plus earnings that have been kept in the company instead of being paid out in dividends. Same as net worth.

SHORT POSITION: The situation in which an investor has sold stock short and has not yet purchased the stock in the open market to replace the borrowed shares.

SHORT SELLING: The selling of a stock that the seller does not own. The stock is typically borrowed from a stockbroker, then sold. At some point in the future the stock must be replaced by purchasing it in the open market.

SIGNATURE GUARANTEE: The guarantee of an investor's signature on a stock certificate by a member of the NYSE or by a commercial bank or a federal savings and loan. The signature on a stock certificate must be signature guaranteed to sell the shares.

SPECIMEN CERTIFICATE: A certificate that was a printer's sample and was never meant to be issued. The word "SPECIMEN" is usually printed across the front of the certificate.

SPREAD: The difference between a stock's bid and ask prices.

STATEMENT OF CHANGES IN FINANCIAL POSITION: Also called a cash flow statement, this statement typically accompanies a balance sheet and income statement in a company's annual report. This statement explains the difference in the amount of cash and cash equivalents the company had at the beginning of the year compared to the end of the year. It shows where the money came from and where the money was spent.

STOCK: Sold in increments called shares, it is a vehicle through which a company can raise money rather than borrowing it. When an investor purchases a company's stock, he or she receives part ownership of the company and derives certain benefits and rights.

STOCK DIVIDEND: A dividend that is paid with additional shares of the company's stock instead of cash. While the shareholders each have more shares than before, each share is worth less in terms of EPS, book value, etc., because the stock has been diluted.

STOCK SPLIT: An increase in the number of shares issued by a company without any change in its financial position. Companies usually do a stock split when their stock price has reached such a high level that the average investor can't afford to purchase it. A two-for-one stock split would reduce the price of a $80 stock to $40.

STOCK SYMBOL: A shortened, usually two-to four-letter, designation that represents a public company. These symbols, instead of the company's full name, are used on a ticker tape.

STOCKBROKER: The person who acts as a liaison between the buyers and sellers of stock. Stockbrokers are also called account executives or registered representatives.

STOP LIMIT ORDER: The same as a stop order, except that when the stock opens a day's trading below the stop limit order price, the stock will not be sold.

STOP ORDER: An order placed with a broker to buy or sell a specific stock when its market price hits a certain point. Using the stop order gives the shareholder the ability to take advantage of any increase in the stock's price, usually without losing the ability to gain at least a certain amount on the sale. If, however, the stock opens a day's trading at below the stop order price, the stock will be sold below the prescribed price.

STRADDLE: The purchase of a put and a call of the same stock, at the same strike price, and with the same expiration date.

STREET NAME ACCOUNT: A brokerage account in which the brokerage firm, not the investor, is listed as the owner. This type of account frees the investor from the responsibility of handling and storing the certificate.

STRIKE PRICE: The preset price at which a call or put gives the investor the option to purchase (call) or sell (put) the stock by a certain date. Also, the preset price at which a Prime stops receiving a stock's price appreciation, and the Score begins receiving any further appreciation. Also called the termination price.

SUPPLY AND DEMAND: The relationship between the amount of goods available and the number of people who want them.

TECHNICAL ANALYSIS: Identifying trends and predicting a stock's price movement through the study of its volume and price in the marketplace.

10-K: An annual financial report a public company is required to file with the Securities and Exchange Commission. Different from the annual report as it contains no frills or pictures and is not used as a marketing tool.

10-Q: A quarterly financial report a public company is required to file with the Securities and Exchange Commission. Different from the quarterly report as it contains no frills or pictures and is not used as a marketing tool.

TENANTS IN COMMON: A form of joint ownership in which people can own unequal amounts of the property held. If one tenant dies, his or her portion of ownership does not automatically go to the other tenant(s). Instead, it is part of the person's estate.

TENDER OFFER: A situation in which a public company offers to buy shares of its stock from current shareholders at a set price. The stock the company buys is called treasury stock. A public company could use this strategy if it wanted to become a private company.

TERMINATION DATE: The preset date on which Scores and Primes and puts and calls expire.

TERMINATION PRICE: See strike price.

THEORY: A speculative plan for predicting the movements of the stock market.

TICKER TAPE: A continuous reporting of stock transactions as they occur with a slight delay. Ticker tapes can be found on certain cable TV stations and in brokerage firm offices.

TRANSFER AGENT: Usually a commercial bank, a transfer agent is an appointed representative of a public company that maintains the company's records of shareholders, issues and cancels stock certificates, pays the dividends, and resolves problems arising from lost, destroyed, or stolen stock certificates.

TRANSPORTATION AVERAGE: Initially called the Railroad Average, it is a mathematical calculation consisting of the prices of twenty transportation stocks that is used as a barometer of the industry.

TREASURY STOCK: Stock that was sold by a public company and subsequently purchased back on the open market.

UNISSUED STOCK: Stock that a public company legally creates, but doesn't sell.

UTILITIES AVERAGE: Developed in 1929, an average of the prices of twenty utility stocks to be used as a barometer of that industry. In 1938, the number of stocks used was reduced to fifteen. The method of calculation has also since been altered.

VIGNETTE: The picture that is printed on the front of a stock certificate. Some certificates are adorned with extremely elaborate vignettes, while others have none at all.

VOLUME: The number of shares changing hands during a trading day. Usually reported in round lots.

WASH SALE RULE: An IRS rule which states that at least thirty days must pass before an investor can repurchase shares sold in order to claim a loss on his or her tax return.

WASTING ASSET: An asset whose value decreases over time until it is virtually worthless, such as a put or a call.

INDEX

{The GLOSSARY is not indexed here as it is alphabetical}

CONSUMER FINANCE BOOKS

THE CONSUMER GUIDE TO VETERAN'S BENEFITS

*Everything You Need to Know to Make the Most of Vetera
Benefits Without Long Lines, the Runaround, and Waitir
on Hold*

United Resource Press

- • There are over 35 million living veterans in the U.S.

The *Consumer Guide to Veteran's Benefits* is the first book
the market to provide up-to-date information on the ent
range of benefits, including disability, home loan guaran
education and training, and employment assistance—more tl
70 benefits explained in all. Addresses and phone numbers fo
service centers nationwide are also included.

A consumer-oriented publishing house, the United Resource
Press was established by Charlene Brown in 1977.

*$7.95, Trade paper, ISBN 0-929230-14-0
Reference, Graphs, Worksheets, 180pp, 5½ x 8½*

United Resource Press

Every benefit available to American veterans, as well as complete application information, is explained in this concise reference guide.

To order this book:

Book Trade ordering:

PUBLISHERS GROUP WEST

4065 Hollis

Emeryville, CA 94608

1-800-365-3453
  (Also available through Ingram)

To order a copy for your library:

QUALITY BOOKS, INC.

918 Sherwood Drive

Lake Bluff, IL 60044-2204

1-708-295-2010

You. may order with your MC/Visa. Call 1-800-637-2256.

Or save $2.00 shipping and handling by sending check or money order to:
United Resource Press, 4521 Campus #388, Irvine, CA 92715. SPECIFY
WHICH BOOK(S) YOU WOULD LIKE.

On prepaid orders shipping and handling is free. Thank you.

CONSUMER FINANCE BOOKS

GUIDE TO SELLING YOUR HOME

Everything You Need to Know to Sell Your Real Estate Without (or With) a Broker in a Competitive Market

Brad G. Greer

- **A money-saving guide to selling a home without having to pay high real-estate commissions**

Home sellers can earn an average of $15,000 by devoting a few hours a week to marketing and selling their own homes. This accessible yet thorough guide shows how to do just that. *Guide to Selling Your Home* inspires, motivates, and gives all necessary information, including: the best time to sell • how to price a home • how to sell if you aren't a natural salesperson • how to host an open house • writing an eye-catching ad • how to review offers • understanding escrow and closing • how to benefit from realtors and still save money.

s Inexpensive, easy-to-
derstand manual can make
ng your home an exciting,
lfying, and very profitable
ture.

Brad G. Greer, a real-estate consultant, lives in Irvine, CA.

$5.95, Trade paper, ISBN 0-929230-07-8
Real Estate, Line drawings, 96pp, 5½ x 8½

United Resource Press

---

order this book:

ok Trade ordering:

JBLISHERS GROUP WEST

65 Hollis

neryville, CA 94608

800-365-3453
(Also available through Ingram)

To order a copy for your library:

QUALITY BOOKS, INC.

918 Sherwood Drive

Lake Bluff, IL 60044-2204

1-708-295-2010

ou may order with your MC/Visa. Call 1-800-637-2256.

save $2.00 shipping and handling by sending check or money order to:
ited Resource Press, 4521 Campus #388, Irvine, CA 92715. SPECIFY
HICH BOOK(S) YOU WOULD LIKE.

prepaid orders shipping and handling is free. Thank you.

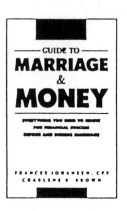

CONSUMER FINANCE BOOKS

THE CONSUMER GUIDE TO COLLEGE FUNDING

Everything You Need to Know to Get College Money:
Investments, Grants, Scholarships and Economical Loans

Edited by Marcia Castaneda

- **Includes detailed information on state and federal funding sources**

An extremely valuable resource in today's world of cutbacks and hard times, this book tells how to apply for and get money for college. It explains everything applicants need to know, from the careful choice of a school to understanding eligibility requirements, meeting deadlines, and qualifying for corporate grants, financial aid, and scholarships.

Marcia Castaneda lives in Laguna Hills, CA.

$7.95, Trade paper, ISBN 0-929230-12-4
Reference/Business, Graphs, 144pp, 5½ x 8½

United Resource Press

oncise, affordable
nce helps college students
nd get the grant and loan
y they need.

order this book:

ok Trade ordering:

BLISHERS GROUP WEST

55 Hollis

eryville, CA 94608

00-365-3453
(Also available through Ingram)

To order a copy for your library:

QUALITY BOOKS, INC.

918 Sherwood Drive

Lake Bluff, IL 60044-2204

1-708-295-2010

u may order with your MC/Visa. Call **1-800-637-2256.**

save $2.00 shipping and handling by sending check or money order to:
ited Resource Press, 4521 Campus #388, Irvine, CA 92715. SPECIFY
IICH BOOK(S) YOU WOULD LIKE.

prepaid orders shipping and handling is free. Thank you.

CONSUMER FINANCE BOOKS

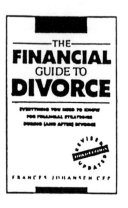

This unique guide walks readers through the financial issues of dissolving a marriage, from the cost of a divorce to making sure a spouse isn't hiding monies.

THE FINANCIAL GUIDE TO DIVORCE

Frances Johansen, CFP

This concise but thorough guide suggests that the best thing a couple can do, once a marriage is over, is to view it as a terminated business partnership. Frances Johansen covers all ficial aspects, including receiving/paying support, determining community property, dividing things fairly, and more. She offeclear explanations and strategies for handling liquid assets, liquid assets and pension funds, taxes, insurance, and living expenses.

Johansen offers advice on budgeting, a handy "Checklist—Preparing for the Divorce, and a glossary of financial terms. She stresses that the property settlement received is the worcapital for a new life—to be assessed and invested wisely.

Frances Johansen lives in Southern California.

$6.95, Trade paper, ISBN 0-929230-03-5
Business/Self-Help, Line drawings, 106pp, 6½ x 8½

To order this book:

Book Trade ordering:

PUBLISHERS GROUP WEST

4065 Hollis

Emeryville, CA 94608

1-800-365-3453
   {Also available through Ingram}

To order a copy for your library:

QUALITY BOOKS, INC.

918 Sherwood Drive

Lake Bluff, IL 60044-2204

1-708-295-2010

<u>You</u> may order with your MC/Visa. Call 1-800-637-2256.

Or save $2.00 shipping and handling by sending check or money order to: United Resource Press, 4521 Campus #388, Irvine, CA 92715. SPECIFY WHICH BOOK{S} YOU WOULD LIKE.

On prepaid orders shipping and handling is free. Thank you.

CONSUMER FINANCE BOOKS

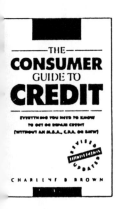

THE CONSUMER GUIDE TO CREDIT

Everything You Need to Know to Get or Repair Credit (Without an M.B.A., C.P.A., or BMW)
Third Edition, Revised and Updated

Charlene B. Brown

- Personal loan criteria and credit protection laws
- What debt collectors can and cannot do
- Home-buying guide

This book helps to clear up misconceptions about banks, credit reporting agencies, loan officers, house buying, and debt collectors. Charlene B. Brown offers practical advice on how the reader can clear credit and be able to buy property, pay off loans, and start treating finances as a business.

Charlene B. Brown is a consumer advocate and lobbyist who teaches seminars on consumer credit. She lives in Aztec, NM.

$5.95, Trade paper, ISBN 0-929230-06-X
Business, 12 line drawings, self-evaluation form, 114pp, 6½ x 8½
United Resource Press

, concise advice on how to
onsumer laws to clear
, work around debt collec-
and get a second chance at
nance game.

order this book:

ok Trade ordering:

BLISHERS GROUP WEST

5 Hollis

eryville, CA 94608

00-365-3453
{Also available through Ingram}

To order a copy for your library:

QUALITY BOOKS, INC.

918 Sherwood Drive

Lake Bluff, IL 60044-2204

1-708-295-2010

u may order with your MC/Visa. Call 1-800-637-2256.

save $2.00 shipping and handling by sending check or money order to:
ited Resource Press, 4521 Campus #388, Irvine, CA 92715. SPECIFY
IICH BOOK{S} YOU WOULD LIKE.

prepaid orders shipping and handling is free. Thank you.

...**BOOKS WORTH READING!**

...seems like the books that are worth reading never find the time to be read...

...the four consumer guides featured in this ad are perfect examples of important books...books filled with helpful, vital information...books that offer you tips on these subjects...**however, if you don't have the time to read these books or just want the information NOW we have a new Consumer Info Line, just for you...**

Guide To Veteran's Benefits: jobs, benefits and other tips to assist veterans.

Consumer Guide to Credit: do it yourself cleaning up your credit, debt and bankruptcy info.

Consumer Guide To College Funding: if you're looking for ways "to get the money to get to college", this is for you.

Consumer Guide To Public Auctions: don't miss another auction...get addressees and tips, have a pencil and paper ready!

...sometimes author, sometimes editor, all the time advocate, Charlene B. Brown invites you to call our new Consumer Info Line to receive this information NOW on the subjects listed above...

CALL

1-900-288-5505